NEW DIRECTIONS FOR ADUL

Susan Imel, *Ohio State Univers*
EDITOR-IN-CHIEF

Adult Learning and the Internet

Brad Cahoon
University of Georgia

EDITOR

Number 78, Summer 1998

JOSSEY-BASS PUBLISHERS
San Francisco

ADULT LEARNING AND THE INTERNET
Brad Cahoon (ed.)
New Directions for Adult and Continuing Education, no. 78
Susan Imel, Editor-in-Chief

ISSN 1052-2891   ISBN 0–7879-1166-6

NEW DIRECTIONS FOR ADULT AND CONTINUING EDUCATION is part of The
Jossey-Bass Higher and Adult Education Series and is published quarterly
by Jossey-Bass Inc., Publishers, 350 Sansome Street, San Francisco, California 94104–1342. Periodicals postage paid at San Francisco, California,
and at additional mailing offices. Postmaster: Send address changes to
New Directions for Adult and Continuing Education, Jossey-Bass Inc.,
Publishers, 350 Sansome Street, San Francisco, California 94104–1342.

SUBSCRIPTIONS cost $54.00 for individuals and $90.00 for institutions,
agencies, and libraries.

EDITORIAL CORRESPONDENCE should be sent to the Editor-in-Chief, Susan
Imel, ERIC/ACVE, 1900 Kenny Road, Columbus, Ohio 43210–1090. E-
mail: imel.1@osu.edu.

Cover photograph by Wernher Krutein/PHOTOVAULT © 1990.

http://www.josseybass.com

Printed in the United States of America on acid-free recycled paper containing 100 percent recovered waste paper, of which at least 20 percent is
postconsumer waste.

CONTENTS

EDITOR'S NOTES

Twentieth-century society has been transformed by a series of dramatic innovations in information technology (Lubar, 1993). But unlike the electronic media that have preceded it, the Internet is beginning to break down the distinctions between providers and consumers of information. The ability to search the terabytes of data that make up the World Wide Web at the click of a mouse is impressive, but it is less revolutionary than the ease with which Internet users can communicate their ideas to each other through e-mail, online conferencing, and Web pages. Combining a global, omnidirectional communications network with the information processing power of computers, the Internet is reshaping our economic life at the same time it is creating new standards of literacy and new forms of culture.

Adult and continuing educators, like their colleagues in other fields, have been quick to sense the potential of the Internet to change almost every aspect of their practice. While some may hail the new technologies as the key to reforming and revitalizing educational institutions, others may wonder uneasily what place current institutions will find on the Internet. Millions of adults have already put themselves on-line, and millions more will follow (Graphics, Visualization, and Usability Center, 1998). In this dynamic environment, educators must ask not only how the Internet can be used to teach, but how the social structures of traditional schooling can adapt to technologies that are redistributing information and the power to access it.

The purpose of this sourcebook is to explore the effects of the Internet on adult learning—both as that learning is facilitated through formal instruction and as it occurs spontaneously in the experiences of individuals and groups—and to provide guidance to adult and continuing educators searching for ways to use the Internet more effectively in their practice. Taken as a whole, the sourcebook provides a thorough survey of the research literature. The chapters also reflect the hard-won personal experiences of the authors, all of whom are directly involved in the use of Internet technologies to facilitate adult learning.

In the opening chapter, I draw on research in human-computer interaction to describe the nature of Internet skills and the cognitive and social processes through which adults learn them. This provides a theoretical context for a description of the teaching methods used in a successful noncredit short course, "Exploring the Internet."

Chapter Two focuses on the use of Internet technologies within the organizational networks known as *intranets*. In her review of research, Linda Gilbert shows how intranets can reduce training costs by providing just-in-time learning and performance support. This chapter also describes the shifting balance between human knowledge and the logic and information embedded in software, which may require us to reconsider our ideas about the division of labor between people and computers.

The next four chapters focus on the use of the Internet in traditional educational settings, dealing with the design of instructional Web resources, the characteristics of adult distance learners, group learning in on-line conferences, and the organization and administration of on-line education. In Chapter Three, Kathleen King provides practical guidelines for educators who want to develop their own Web-based course materials, reviewing the instructional capabilities of various web technologies and posing questions about curriculum, construction, and evaluation that can guide practitioners through the development process.

Adult learners and their interactions with different levels of Internet-based distance education are the subject of Chapter Four. Daniel Eastmond presents a typology of distance learning models arranged along a continuum of technological sophistication and shows how each model can be used to support specific characteristics of adult learning.

On-line conferences and discussion groups are among the most powerful instructional tools offered by the Internet, but such virtual communities present facilitators with unique challenges. In Chapter Five, Margaret Holt, Pamela Kleiber, Jill Swenson, Frances Rees, and Judy Milton summarize their findings about the facilitation of group learning on the Internet, based on a three-year series of on-line National Issues Forums.

In Chapter Six, Lynne Schrum looks at the issues facing educators and institutions as they plan, provide, and support on-line education. An overview of research on pedagogical, organizational, and institutional issues suggests methods for the production and delivery of Internet-based courses.

The hyperbole surrounding adult learning and the Internet sometimes tends to obscure troubling ethical concerns. In Chapter Seven, Margaret Holt raises questions of power, equity, access, and privacy that have always been central to educational practice but that take on new dimensions through the mediation of technology.

In the final chapter, I summarize common themes from the other chapters and discuss how emerging Internet technologies may influence adult learning in the twenty-first century.

Any book about the Internet risks obsolescence before it even reaches print. Fortunately, the technology itself offers a partial solution to this dilemma. Hosted by the University of Georgia Center for Continuing Education, the "Adult Learning and the Internet" Web site provides links to most of the Internet resources cited in each chapter, as well as other materials provided by the authors. Readers are invited to share their own experiences and ideas. The site is accessible at http://www.gactr.uga.edu/internet/.

Brad Cahoon
Editor

References

Graphics, Visualization, and Usability Center. WWW User Surveys. [http://www.gvu.gat-ech.edu/user_surveys/]. Atlanta: Georgia Institute of Technology, 1998.

Lubar, S. *InfoCulture: The Smithsonian Book of the Inventions of the Information Age.* Boston: Houghton Mifflin, 1993.

BRAD CAHOON is the Webmaster and coordinator of computer training at the University of Georgia Center for Continuing Education, Athens.

Effective educational uses of the Internet require that teachers and students first learn basic Internet skills. This chapter describes how adults learn to use the Internet and offers guidelines for instruction.

Teaching and Learning Internet Skills

Brad Cahoon

Recently, an older colleague told me he was finally convinced that all the hype surrounding the Internet is true. "I've started getting e-mail from my mother," he said, unable to conceal his incredulity. "If my mother is on the Internet, everybody is going to be on the Internet."

The explosive growth of the Internet is evidence of an extraordinary adult learning phenomenon that cuts across traditional demographic lines. Unlike most of the chapters in this volume, this one does not discuss the Internet as a medium for learning and teaching, but instead focuses on how adults learn to participate in this phenomenon, whether on their own, at work, or through continuing education.

Surveys of Internet usage are subject to a certain amount of methodological controversy (Hoffman, Kalsbeek, and Novak, 1996), but some trends are clear. According to researchers conducting World Wide Web user surveys at Georgia Tech, thirty-six million people in the United States were on the Internet in November, 1997 (Graphics, Visualization, and Usability Center, 1997). Since the user surveys began in 1994, the average age of respondents has steadily increased; in the most recent survey it was thirty-five. About 37 percent of respondents were novices who had been on-line less than one year. Among females, the percentage of novices was 43 percent, while among users older than fifty, 53 percent had gone on-line for the first time within the last twelve months.

Two inferences can be drawn from these and other survey data. First, as it grows, the population of the Internet is becoming increasingly diverse and more consistent with the characteristics of the general population. Once the private domain of a small number of researchers and academics, the Internet has become a true mass medium. Second, this continuous growth means that a large proportion of Internet users are novices. Over the course of the next

NEW DIRECTIONS FOR ADULT AND CONTINUING EDUCATION, no. 78, Summer 1998 © Jossey-Bass Publishers

decade, as Internet technologies achieve a ubiquity comparable to that of the telephone and television, the absolute number of new users will steadily increase—and with it the demand for new resources for teaching and learning Internet skills. This new audience is already creating opportunities and challenges for adult educators, many of whom are learning to use the Internet themselves at the same time they are being asked to provide instruction.

The research literature on general computer skill learning is fairly extensive (Cahoon, 1995; Gattiker, 1992), and has produced some valuable instructional design strategies (Carroll, 1990). In comparison, research about how people learn to use the Internet is still rare. This chapter draws on research in computer and Internet skill learning as well as on interviews with computer workshop instructors and participants to present an overview of the cognitive and social factors that influence the development of Internet skills. This provides the context for a discussion of a successful noncredit short course, "Exploring the Internet," offered by the University of Georgia Center for Continuing Education since 1994. In addition to providing a possible model for other providers of Internet instruction, this example illustrates the techniques used by an expert computer instructor to achieve a balance between hands-on laboratory exercises and verbal presentation of concepts and principles.

Overview of Internet Skills

The pace of innovation on the Internet is so dizzying that any attempt to define a set of core skills may be obsolete by the time it reaches print. Experimental studies by Senkevitch and Wolfram (1997) and Ratner (1998), while useful, suffer from the warping effect of "Web time"—the software they assess had all but disappeared from general use by the time their articles were published. The following description is framed in deliberately general terms to extend its applicability.

Basic personal computer skills are prerequisite to using the Internet, though in practice these skills are often acquired together, as the popularity of the Internet motivates many adults to use computers for the first time. Motor skills (learning to use a keyboard, learning to manipulate a mouse) and perceptual skills (learning to associate images and events on the computer screen with motor actions) form the most elementary substrate. On this basis, adult learners gradually build the skills required by the now-standard graphical user interface: pointing at and clicking on icons to activate programs; selecting commands from pull-down menus; and opening, closing, moving, resizing, and scrolling windows. Once learned, these skills can be applied to a range of software tasks. Other skills that can be transferred easily from one task to another include the use of the mouse to edit text and the use of menu commands to create, save, and print documents.

Skill learning is strongly correlated with the duration and frequency of practice, while skill transfer from one task to another depends on the presence of common elements between those tasks (Singley and Anderson, 1989). For example, the cut-and-paste operations of word processing depend on the learner's recognition and manipulation of elements such as the pointer, insertion point, scrolling windows, and displayed text; all these elements are also present in e-mail programs, so a learner familiar with word processing can apply the same skills to e-mail tasks immediately.

Having acquired a functional set of skills, computer users tend to rely on them heavily, even when they are aware that they could learn more efficient procedures for achieving the same results (Santhanam and Wiedenbeck, 1993). For example, longtime users of word processing software who learned initially to rely on arrow keys to move the cursor within a document may continue to employ this method even though the same goal could be accomplished more efficiently by using the mouse. In some respects, learners who have already achieved a plateau of computer skill may be more difficult to teach than complete novices.

At one level, Internet skills can be described as the ability to use a variety of Internet client software, particularly Web browsers, e-mail programs, news readers, and FTP (file transfer protocol) clients. A skillful Internet user can be operationally defined as one who is able to send and reply to e-mail, search for and find Web information, download and install software from on-line archives, and participate in Web-based conferences or newsgroups. But successful application of these skills to real-world situations requires conceptual understanding as well as the memorization of step-by-step procedures. Brandt (1997) reflects a consensus among cognitive scientists and software engineers when he describes Internet skill learning in terms of the construction of mental models that allow the learner to reason about problems, predict probable events, and discover solutions.

The Internet is a much larger and more complex problem domain than a personal computer. Novice computer users, who are still coming to grips with the concepts of files and directories and with the skills necessary to store and find information on a disk, are easily overwhelmed by the difficulty of searching for information on the Internet, where response times and other forms of feedback are far less consistent and where an overall hierarchical organization is lacking. The cognitive load of Internet use is increased by the hypertext properties of the World Wide Web. While associative linking can support learning in many ways, its potential for creating disorientation has long been recognized (Conklin, 1987).

Successful mental models of the Internet allow learners to reason about the spatial and temporal distribution of both hardware and humans and the means by which they communicate with each other. Some knowledge of the cultural history of the Internet sheds much light on its technical and social organization (Hafner and Lyon, 1996) and is one of the most obvious differences between experts and novices.

The technical success of the Internet is the result of widespread acceptance of public, freely reproducible software protocols such as TCP/IP (Transmission Control Protocol/Internet Protocol). Understanding the complexities of TCP/IP is much less relevant to practical Internet skill than is a basic understanding of client-server computing. All Internet-based communication depends on client software (such as e-mail and Web browser programs) that exchange information with server software on distant computers (such as e-mail and Web servers). This exchange relies on the addressing, routing, and error-correction schemes built into TCP/IP.

By explaining how requests from clients and responses from servers are routed over the Internet, instructors can help learners form realistic expectations and strategies for problem solving. For example, the error messages displayed by a Web browser when it fails to connect to a server can be a source of confusion to novices. A mental model of the Internet that explains how Web clients and servers communicate can support an appropriate response (such as canceling the error message and trying to contact the server again).

Novice users also benefit greatly by acquiring models of the social organization of the Internet. Accustomed to traditional print and broadcast media, in which the flow of information is centrally controlled and one-directional, they tend to find the diversity of the Internet baffling. In time, however, they understand that Internet servers are operated by a variety of people and organizations, each with unique resources and agendas. More experienced users, who have watched the Internet evolve over years or decades, have models of this social structure that help them analyze the relative value of information sources.

Internet users learn skills in response to situational needs. A distinction can be drawn between those who use the Internet primarily at work, relying on e-mail, the Web, and other resources for job-related tasks, and those who use it recreationally with a home computer and an account from an Internet service provider. The two categories often overlap, with home Internet use becoming an increasingly common method of telecommuting, but an important difference is that the home user must learn to do his or her own technical troubleshooting, rather than relying on network support staff. Installing a modem, configuring software, and solving connection problems are nontrivial tasks, especially for novices. Nonetheless, large numbers of people who do not work with networked computers—many of them older adults—are logging on to the Internet as recreational users, often motivated by the desire to use e-mail to communicate with family and friends. Whether at home or at work, the social contexts of Internet use tend to determine what skills novices will learn and how.

Strategies for Learning and Teaching Internet Skills

Typically, adults gain Internet skills through some combination of self-directed learning, informal learning within a work group, and participation in workshops or short courses.

A flood of newspaper articles, books, and magazines indicates that old-fashioned paper is still a viable tool for learning about the Internet. Many adults, particularly those who use the Internet at home, rely on computer books as their main resource for solving problems. An enormous variety of self-instructional material is also available on the World Wide Web, much of it aimed at novices (for example, Cahoon, 1997). More experienced Internet users often use search engines to scour the Web, Usenet, and mailing list archives for answers to obscure technical questions. However, successful use of such resources presupposes significant prior knowledge.

For those who use Internet tools in an office setting, informal knowledge sharing with coworkers is often more important than any type of formal instruction, whether individualized or instructor-led. Typically, such informal learning experiences involve the identification of specific work group members as local experts, the tacit or explicit negotiation of roles for shared computer work, and one-on-one problem-solving or tutoring sessions (Cahoon, 1995, 1996). This knowledge sharing is especially effective because it can be requested on a just-in-time basis and occurs within a mutually understood context of work goals and resources. Such situated learning involves processes of socialization as well as the mastery of concepts and procedures (Lave and Wegner, 1991). However, it can be costly in the demands placed on the time of local experts, and it may not occur at all within work groups whose culture emphasizes strong distinctions of status and authority. For example, in organizations where all computer tasks are delegated to clerical staff, managers may have few opportunities for informal learning.

Participation in short courses and workshops is an increasingly popular method for novices to develop basic Internet skills in a relatively short period of time. However, such courses seem to vary significantly in their effectiveness. The determinative factor is often not the technical expertise of the instructor but the selection of teaching strategies that combine an emphasis on practical exercises with an opportunistic approach to the verbal presentation of concepts and principles.

"Exploring the Internet"

"Exploring the Internet," a ten-hour noncredit evening class, was first taught at the University of Georgia Center for Continuing Education in February 1994. Offered three to four times a year since then, it receives steady enrollment and positive participant evaluations. Its goal is to provide adult novices with the concepts and skills necessary to use the Web, e-mail, and other Internet tools. The course is taught in a Windows computer lab with a computer for each student as well as one for the instructor. The lab has a projection system to display the instructor's screen, and all the computers have direct network connections to the Internet.

The course is frequently taught by Darrell Rainey, a graphic designer who works for the university. Like many of the computer instructors who teach for the Georgia Center, Darrell does not have an academic background in computer science or engineering. This is an advantage for him, as the program planners have discovered that teachers with deep technical expertise tend to be less effective in communicating with novices than experienced computer users from other backgrounds. The following description of "Exploring the Internet," its participants, and the activities and teaching strategies that have made it a success is based on interviews with Darrell and observations of his classes.

The course description specifies that experience with basic mouse and keyboard use is required, and in general participants meet this prerequisite, but otherwise they are a diverse group, varying widely in age, prior computer experience, and educational backgrounds. Darrell estimates that as many as half of the participants in recent classes had Internet access at home during the time they were enrolled, something that was rare when the first class was offered. Couples, parents and children, and friends often take the course together. Asked at the beginning of the class to describe their reasons for taking it, many allude to relationships rather than work requirements, citing children or spouses who already use the Internet. Other participants are small-business owners or employees interested in using the Internet for communicating with customers.

The class is taught in five two-hour sessions. Typically Darrell spends one hour of each session teaching Web skills and the other hour working with e-mail, FTP, or newsgroups. One of the most striking characteristics of his teaching style is his avoidance of lecturing. The main exception is the first session, which he begins by introducing himself, surveying the participants about their goals and previous experience, and presenting a brief overview of the history of the Internet and some basic concepts of client-server computing. Within the first half-hour, he has begun to lead the group through hands-on exercises. His subsequent presentation of conceptual material is done almost entirely through responses to questions and especially through his interventions to resolve students' problems.

A typical activity in the first session involves learning to use Netscape Navigator to retrieve a Web page by entering its address. Taking the White House Web site at http://www.whitehouse.gov/ as an example, Darrell demonstrates how to reach the Web site, explaining each step of the procedure as the students observe his actions on the projection screen. He then calls on them to repeat the process themselves. Most students are able to do so, but inevitably several will fail, receiving error messages or other unexpected results.

Where a less experienced computer instructor might view these errors as disruptive of the flow of the class, and either ignore or hurry past them, Darrell uses them as opportunities to demonstrate troubleshooting skills and to present or reinforce conceptual information. Asking the participant to describe the symptoms of the problem to the rest of the group, Darrell identifies its source—in the case of this exercise, often a simple typing error—and explains the often-cryptic error messages. An error reporting a failure to resolve a domain name might lead him to provide a brief explanation of the purpose and format of domain names. Then he suggests steps for recovering from the error (for example, canceling an error message and correcting a mistyped Web address). Darrell's primary goal is to give his students experience in overcoming errors. The effectiveness of this strategy is demonstrated by students' progress in the class and their positive self-assessments in course evaluations.

This focus on error recovery, which has support in the experimental work of Carroll (1990), benefits students in two ways. First, by moving students quickly into hands-on exercises and then using errors as opportunities to explain concepts, Darrell provides a practical context for material that might be confusing or boring if delivered as part of an extended lecture. Computer errors are events that are both memorable and likely to recur; by associating the explanation with the experience of an error, Darrell increases the likelihood that the student will recall both the solution and its rationale under similar circumstances. Second, through his relaxed approach to hardware crashes, software failures, and network outages, Darrell demonstrates that troubleshooting episodes are a normal part of using the Internet and models the attitudes and tactics necessary to resolve them. While this method of instruction is less systematic than detailed, organized lecturing, in practice it allows students to construct and retain more reliable mental models.

Darrell uses similar approaches in teaching his students to use e-mail. During the class, each student has access to a temporary e-mail account. Prior to a class session, Darrell sends brief messages to the students, who read and reply to them during the class. He then randomly distributes index cards on which he has written the students' e-mail addresses and has participants exchange messages with each other. To show the kinds of errors produced by defective e-mail addresses, Darrell deliberately sends mail to a nonexistent account on the local mail server (such as "bogus@gactr.uga.edu"), then to a nonexistent server (such as "bogus@bogus.edu"). Discussion of the different messages produced by these errors deepens students' understanding of the interactions of client and server programs on the Internet.

However, not all concepts are best conveyed through analysis of errors. In some instances, the social consequences of errors make it desirable to avoid them. For example, teaching students about mailing lists requires both a series of activities—in which students subscribe to a list, read mail, and unsubscribe from the list—and a brief lecture about the etiquette of mailing list participation. Darrell urges students to postpone participation in lists until they have read others' messages for some time and have consulted available FAQs (frequently asked question documents). Similarly, Darrell discusses flaming (exchanges of angry or abusive e-mail) and recommends that students wait to mail any particularly heated comments.

At the end of the ten-hour course, most students report that they feel confident in their ability to apply what they have learned and to continue to develop their skills on their own, using the textbook provided in the class as well as information they find on the Web.

Conclusion

The rapid evolution of Internet technologies is likely to accelerate, complicating the teaching and learning of Internet skills. As more powerful protocols replace older ones, whole areas of curricula can quickly become obsolete. One example is Gopher, which was the preferred method of publishing documents on the Internet in 1994 but which has since been largely replaced by the World Wide Web. In turn, as Web browsers have become standard, software vendors have added new capabilities to them, increasing their complexity. It seems clear that, in its turn, today's Web will be replaced by technologies better suited to a faster, more media-rich Internet.

Given the certainty of technological change, even experienced Internet users face the need for continuous learning. Adult educators can prepare students for this experience by helping them construct mental models that support experimentation and problem solving. The most durable of these models will emphasize understanding the Internet as a social environment rather than knowledge about computers and cables.

References

Brandt, D. S. "Constructivism: Teaching for Understanding of the Internet." *Communications of the ACM,* 1997, *40*(10), 112–117.

Cahoon, B. "Computer Skill Learning in the Workplace." Unpublished doctoral dissertation, Department of Adult Education, University of Georgia, 1995.

Cahoon, B. "Group Learning and Technology." In S. Imel (ed.), *Learning in Groups: Exploring Fundamental Principles, New Uses, and Emerging Opportunities.* New Directions for Adult and Continuing Education, no. 71. San Francisco: Jossey-Bass, 1996.

Cahoon, B. "Exploring the World-Wide Web." [http://www.gactr.uga.edu/exploring/]. Feb. 1997.

Carroll, J. M. *The Nurnberg Funnel: Designing Minimalist Instruction for Practical Computer Skill.* Cambridge, Mass.: MIT Press, 1990.

Conklin, E. J. "Hypertext: An Introduction and a Survey." *IEEE Computer,* 1987, *20*, 17–41.

Gattiker, U. E. "Computer Skills Acquisition: A Review and Future Directions for Research." *Journal of Management,* 1992, *18*, 547–574.

Graphics, Visualization, and Usability Center. WWW User Surveys. [http://www.gvu.gatech.edu/user_surveys/]. Atlanta: Georgia Institute of Technology, 1998.

Hafner, K., and Lyon, M. *Where Wizards Stay Up Late: The Origins of the Internet.* New York: Simon & Schuster, 1996.

Hoffman, D. L., Kalsbeek, W. D., and Novak, T. P. "Internet and Web Use in the United States: Baselines for Commercial Development." [http://www2000.ogsm.vanderbilt.edu/baseline/internet.demos.july9.1996.html]. Nashville, Tenn.: Project 2000, Owen Graduate School of Management, Vanderbilt University, July 1996.

Lave, J., and Wegner, E. *Situated Learning: Legitimate Peripheral Participation.* New York: Cambridge University Press, 1991.

Ratner, J. "Easing the Learning Curve for Novice Web Users." In C. Forsythe, E. Grose, and J. Ratner (eds.), *Human Factors and Web Development.* Mahwah, N.J.: Erlbaum, 1998.

Santhanam, R., and Wiedenbeck, S. "Neither Novice nor Expert: The Discretionary User of Software." *International Journal of Man-Machine Studies,* 1993, *38*, 201–229.

Senkevitch, J. J., and Wolfram, D. "Internetworking an Urban Community: A Longitudinal Study of Approaches to Introducing Adult New Users to Electronic Information Resources." *Library & Information Science Research,* 1997, *19*(3), 249–264.

Singley, M. K., and Anderson, J. R. *The Transfer of Cognitive Skill.* Cambridge, Mass.: Harvard University Press, 1989.

BRAD CAHOON is the Webmaster and coordinator of computer instruction at the University of Georgia Center for Continuing Education, Athens.

This chapter discusses the potential of intranets for transforming the learning process, including design and implementation issues.

Intranets for Learning and Performance Support

Linda S. Gilbert

At Company A, Michael checks his calendar and groans. The half-day training session on interviewing skills scheduled for this week involves two hours of travel to the central office. He resents the time lost, especially since he only hires a few people each year. By next time, he'll have forgotten everything he learned.

At Company B, Jenny checks her calendar and notices that she has interviews scheduled later in the week. It's been a while since she filled a position, so she logs on to her company's intranet to review a training module on interviewing. She skims most of the sections, concentrating on the few she truly needs. Jenny also downloads a "job aid"—a list of questions that she can use during the interview. Without leaving her desk, she's prepared for the week.

This scenario illustrates the potential that intranets have to transform the learning process. What exactly are intranets, and how are they being used for learning and performance support?

Intranet Structure and Use

The term *intranet* refers both to the technical infrastructure—the physical connections between computers—and to the total collection of software and information made available through that infrastructure. Technically, an intranet is simply an internal corporate or organizational network, over which information and programs can be shared by multiple users. A *firewall* or security system allows entry to authorized users only, creating a bounded system.

NEW DIRECTIONS FOR ADULT AND CONTINUING EDUCATION, no. 78, Summer 1998 © Jossey-Bass Publishers

Intranets allow users to share files and programs, access information, and communicate with one another electronically. These capabilities have tremendous potential for organizations on a number of levels, including training and performance support.

This chapter will review the technical aspects of intranets, but will primarily focus on intranet-based training and performance support systems and their implications for adult learning.

Technical Infrastructure. Intranets use the same networking protocols as the public Internet (for example, TCP/IP, SMTP, and HTTP). The primary difference is that an intranet is only available to certain users who have been authorized to access it. These boundaries make it possible to describe an intranet in terms of size, scope, hardware and software, and even user characteristics. Like the Internet, intranets predate World Wide Web technology, but their use expanded exponentially once the Web developed. Though an intranet is not necessarily Web-based, the term often refers to internal networks that publish information on Web servers for access with Web browsers.

The technical advantages of delivering learning and performance support over an intranet include ease of distribution, ease of access, and use of existing infrastructure. These advantages offer immediate cost savings, as well as the promise of transforming work and learning as a result of increased connectivity.

Ease of Distribution. Distributing software and information through an intranet saves duplication, shipping, and other distribution costs. In addition, since shared resources can be reached by anyone on the intranet, each user's individual storage space ceases to be a limiting factor.

Ease of distribution affects not only the initial circulation of software or information but also subsequent maintenance. The original can be updated easily from a central location, alleviating concerns that users may be operating with outdated information, programs, or procedures. Centralized distribution is a genuine advantage for version control, cost savings, and timeliness of information.

An intranet may solve some distribution problems, but it creates others. First, users may not use all the resources they should. Though newer technologies *push* information to the user (that is, they supply information to the user's computer without a specific request from the user), most intranets still rely on users *pulling* (requesting) the material they need. Distribution issues have thus widened from making sure that resources are physically available to attracting the user to them. Second, although the information or program may be easily updated, the ability to access it may not keep pace. Available technology changes rapidly, and not every user within an organization is likely to be able to follow the changes at the same rate. This leads to the issue of access.

Ease of Access. One of the major strengths of intranets is that users can share programs, information, and tools across different computer systems and configurations. This ease of access makes it possible to create a network open to everyone in the organization.

However, technical accessibility is far from uniform. Standards are still evolving, so compatibility between different computer systems holds for only the most basic files. Even simple graphics can vary from computer to computer. Similar computers may be running different configurations of programs, such as the Web plug-ins that extend the functionality of browsers. Further, in large organizations, the cost of equipment replacement ensures that not all computer users will have the most current hardware. In terms of design, these technical constraints mean that audio, video, and downloadable files may not be available to all the end users. Designers have to balance high-end functionality against access issues.

Use of Existing Infrastructure. Use of existing network connections and computers is considered a particularly strong advantage for intranets, particularly for Web-based intranets. The architecture of the Web offers a nonproprietary system that is familiar to most users. Multiple providers for components mean that pricing is competitive and that companies need not fear investing in a dead-end technology.

At the same time, this open architecture makes decisions about hardware and software more complex. Different components may not work together as expected and can require laborious research and troubleshooting. The rapid pace of technological development makes system maintenance a moving target. To use the current infrastructure, some functions available on stand-alone systems have to be reconsidered. For example, network bandwidth limitations still hamper implementation of real-time audio or video over an intranet, which in turn limits the use of existing computer-based training that requires multimedia.

While it is true that recent advances continue to make intranet technology far more feasible, maintaining and selecting an appropriate system requires effort, expense, and expertise.

Learning and Performance Support. Although critical, technical considerations are only a small part of the picture. The value of an intranet lies in its content and use. Intranets permit just-in-time or on-demand training on an individual basis through improved delivery of learning resources. They also promote the development of shared resources and collaborative work practices.

Review of Learning and Performance Resources. Intranet resources include adaptations of existing, non-networked resources, such as information from printed materials, computer-based training, and electronic performance support systems.

The term *computer-based training* describes the delivery system more than the instructional content. Traditional computer-based training usually consists of tutorials, drills, simulations, or instructional games. However, computers are also being used to build more open-ended *learning environments* to encourage exploration and problem solving (Alessi and Trollip, 1991; Cognition and Technology Group at Vanderbilt, 1991; De Grave, Boshuizen, and Schmidt, 1996; Goodrum, Dorsey, and Schwen, 1993). Descriptions of such learning environments tend to merge with those of electronic performance support systems (EPSS).

The primary difference between a learning environment and an electronic performance support system is that the focus of an EPSS is not learning, per se: an EPSS represents a blend of learning and work, with an emphasis on performance as the ultimate goal (Rosenberg, 1995). Since individuals can access updated information and procedures when they need them, some learning becomes unnecessary. For example, an EPSS for a chair manufacturer might include a database containing colors, styles, and prices that users can access when talking to a customer. Instead of memorizing all the options that are available, salespeople can concentrate on finding combinations that fit the customer's needs. Using performance support to minimize rote learning in this way reduces information overload for workers and allows them to concentrate on higher cognitive processes.

A number of interrelated fields contribute to perspectives on EPSS: performance technology, instructional technology, knowledge engineering, information engineering, business process reengineering, and systems thinking (Laffey, 1995; Raybould, 1995; Rosenberg, 1995). Initial developers of electronic performance support systems conceived an EPSS as an electronic system that provided integrated, on-demand access to information, advice, learning experiences, examples, and tools to enable a high level of job performance with a minimum of support from other people (Gery, 1991). The goal of an EPSS is "to provide whatever is necessary to generate performance and learning at the moment of need" (Gery, 1991, p. 34).

Current definitions of electronic performance support systems have shifted their focus from specific components to overall impact. Performance-centered design is usually cited as one of the hallmarks of an EPSS (Gery, 1995a; Laffey, 1995; McGraw, 1997; Raybould, 1995, 1997). Performance-centered design reflects the user's goals within a work environment, communicating what the user needs to do to achieve those goals and providing support in carrying out the associated tasks (Dickelman, 1995; McGraw, 1997; Norman, 1993). In addition to making the right tool available at the right time, a good performance system clarifies relationships, sequences, priorities, decisions, and standards related to the task (Gery, 1995b; McGraw, 1995; Raybould, 1995; Rosenberg, 1995).

In practice, performance and learning are so deeply interconnected that systems designed for performance support often support learning as well. Situating information and learning resources in a work context provides a natural way for learning to take place, especially since adults are usually task-centered, self-directed learners (Dorsey, Goodrum, and Schwen, 1993; Duchastel and Lang, 1995–96; Ference and Vockell, 1994; Merriam, 1993; Schwen, Goodrum, and Dorsey, 1993; Wilson, 1993). Nonetheless, EPSS development has been driven by businesses rather than by educational institutions (Hudzina, Rowley, and Wager, 1996).

Advocates of performance support systems—a term that includes learning experiences such as computer-based training—identify advantages for both individuals and organizations. Table 2.1 summarizes some of the major benefits cited for each.

Table 2.1. Advantages of Performance Support Systems

For Individuals	For Organizations
• Access to information bases	• Consistent training
• Just-in-time, on-demand learning experiences, focused on user's needs	• Reduced travel costs
	• Procedural consistency
• Access to procedural guidance (job aids, checklists, and so on)	• Rapid performance for novices
• Collection of tools, templates, and guidance to support performance	
• User selection of resources and strategies	
• Reduced demands on memory	
• Situated learning in task context	

For individuals, just-in-time access to information, tools, and training enables them to focus on their goals. Without the demands of a class schedule, individuals can linger on unfamiliar material and not waste time on things they already know. Users select the resources that they need, so individuals can customize their use of the system.

For organizations, on-demand training reduces travel time and increases the applicability of learning to the individual's needs and immediate situation. These factors improve productivity while lowering training costs. Performance support tools and templates also allow less experienced workers to perform more advanced tasks than they would ordinarily be capable of, so that more experienced—and higher-paid—workers can concentrate on tasks where their specific expertise is required (Thomas, Baron, and Schmidt, 1994).

Advantages of Intranet Connections. The advantages of stand-alone training or performance support systems are enhanced by placing them on an intranet. A connected system can not only facilitate individual learning but ensure that new knowledge is captured, recorded, and made available to others in the organization (Laffey, 1995; Raybould, 1995; Rosenberg, 1995).

The immediate implications of intranet connections are that all the components of a performance support system—training, information, tools, and other resources—can be consistent, up to date, and available from any individual's workstation. Performance support using Web technology offers the additional advantage of a consistent and familiar interface, reducing cognitive load.

At the same time that an intranet allows more access to existing resources, it usually leads to the creation of more resources. Web pages are not difficult to produce, and departments may choose electronic publishing for information once distributed in print: reports and updates, company handbooks and policies, organizational charts, and so forth. They may also create resources for their workers and internal clients and share them with others in the organization.

From this array, users acquire the resources they need, tailoring their collections in much the same way they customize their workspaces (Sherry and Wilson, 1996).

For the organization, the scope of electronic performance support systems can be enlarged to include entire work groups, sometimes in ways that transform their tasks (Laffey, 1995; Raybould, 1995; Rosenberg, 1995; Ryder and Wilson, 1996; Scales and Yang, 1993; Thomas, Baron, and Schmidt, 1994). Collaborative group work can be better supported, leading to increased sharing of information between users. For example, imagine a computer-repair company that has technical engineering support in different geographical regions. If the engineers can add new problems and solutions to a shared database, they can draw on the expertise of all their colleagues to solve problems instead of locally reinventing the solution everywhere the same problem appears. Thus, as members of an organization learn, their new knowledge can become part of the performance support system, disseminated to others who can use it. *Dynamic EPSS* is one name for a performance support system to which users contribute (Laffey, 1995). Instead of delivering a static performance support system, the intranet becomes an evolving performance support system composed of shared resources distributed throughout the organization.

Concerns and Issues

The explosion of new resources supported by an intranet can be a tremendous advantage to individuals and organizations. It can also be a tremendous disadvantage, contributing to information overload. Problems occur when the key characteristics that define a true performance support system—performance-centered design and integration with the working environment—are neglected during resource development and overall system design. Unbridled development and lack of organization can lead to fragmented and poorly utilized resources.

The value of an intranet depends on three factors: the individual quality of the resources; the degree to which they are maintained; and the ease with which the users can find, select, and use them. Resources are sometimes developed without adequate consideration of the users' needs and working environment. Once developed, they may not be adequately updated, so that they become unreliable. And even when adequately maintained, they may be fragmented and hard to find; separate resources need to be integrated into an overall system, particularly in larger intranets where locating information becomes a challenge.

Factors external to the system may affect its impact as well. Users may lack skills for choosing among the resources appropriately. More significantly, organizational policies, procedures, or culture can create unexpected barriers. Imbalances between individual and organizational needs—for example, systems that simplify processes to the point that they deskill workers—are also a major concern (Clark, 1992; Hudzina, Rowley, and Wager, 1996; Nickerson, 1993; Salomon, 1993; Scales and Yang, 1993).

Successful implementation of an intranet depends on thoughtful initial assessment, a wide array of development expertise, a commitment to maintenance, and iterative evaluation and redesign. In addition, it usually requires attention to the larger organizational context. It may include strategies such as training in its use, modification of policies and procedures, and alignment of individual and organizational incentives (Clark, 1992; Kling and Jewett, 1994; Nickerson, 1993; Sherry and Wilson, 1996). Processes that stress iterative design, incremental development, regular evaluation, and participation from the end users improve chances of success (Laffey, 1995; Raybould, 1995).

Implications for Adult Learning

On the surface, working with well-designed performance support systems satisfies many of the conditions conducive to adult learning. Characteristics of adult learners include an independent self-concept, a background of prior experience, a natural orientation toward learning, and strong internal motivation (Pratt, 1993). Recent theories involving the context of learning suggest that learning is to some extent situation-specific; thus, work provides a natural setting for adult learning (Brown, Collins, and Duguid, 1989; Dorsey, Goodrum, and Schwen, 1993; Goodrum, Dorsey, and Schwen, 1993; Lave and Wegner, 1991; Wilson, 1993). As users call on the resources of the system to achieve their goals, they have the opportunity to build their expertise.

However, such learning is not a given. It requires not only experience but reflection (Schön, 1983). Intranet users may not have the time, energy, or personal motivation to pursue learning; they may simply choose to get their work done as quickly as possible. In addition, novices are often unable to accurately assess their learning needs or the strategies to best fulfill them. Moreover, a system may be designed so that human skills are undeveloped (Salomon, 1993; Scales and Yang, 1993).

As technology increasingly supports knowledge work, one of the most critical decisions involves distinguishing situations in which learning is desirable from those in which it represents unnecessary effort (Brown, Collins, and Duguid, 1989; Clark, 1992, 1995; De Grave, Boshuizen, and Schmidt, 1996; Ference and Vockell, 1994; Scales and Yang, 1993; Wilson, 1993). Identifying what needs to be learned—or not learned—in a technical society is a question with enormous implications for educators.

Users will need help in learning how to best use the resources available to them. To maximize the use of these systems for performance and learning, individuals and work teams need to develop both technical skills and conceptual skills. Supporting performance support involves coaching people in how to use the system and tools effectively (Sherry and Wilson, 1996). At the same time, it involves encouraging reflective practices that allow people to learn from their work activities—and that maximize their ability to learn from performance support systems (Brown, Collins, and Duguid, 1989). As Martin Ryder and Brent Wilson said about the Internet, "Since we can no longer filter and select proper materials for our students, our highest calling as educators will be to support students in developing such discipline for themselves" (Ryder and Wilson, 1996, p. 651). The same is true for intranets and performance support systems.

References

Alessi, S. M., and Trollip, S. R. *Computer-Based Instruction: Methods and Development.* (2nd ed.). Upper Saddle River., N.J.: Prentice Hall, 1991.

Brown, J. S., Collins, A., and Duguid, P. "Situated Cognition and the Culture of Learning." *Educational Researcher,* 1989, *18*(1), 32–42.

Clark, R. C. "EPSS—Look Before You Leap: Some Cautions About Applications of Electronic Performance Support Systems." *Performance and Instruction,* 1992, *31*(5), 22–25.

Clark, R. C. "21st Century Human Performance." *Training,* 1995, *32* (6), 85–90.

Cognition and Technology Group at Vanderbilt. "Technology and the Design of Generative Learning Environments." *Educational Technology,* 1991, *31*(5), 34–40.

De Grave, W. S., Boshuizen, H.P.A., and Schmidt, H. G. "Problem Based Learning: Cognitive and Metacognitive." *Instructional Science,* 1996, *24*(5), 321–41.

Dickelman, G. J. "Things That Help Us Perform: Reviewing Ideas from Donald Norman." *Performance Improvement Quarterly,* 1995, *8*(1), 23–30.

Dorsey, L. T., Goodrum, D. A., and Schwen, T. M. "Just-in-Time Knowledge Performance Support: A Test of Concept." *Educational Technology,* Nov. 1993, pp. 21–29.

Duchastel, P., and Lang, J. "Performance Support Systems for Learning." *Journal of Educational Technology Systems,* 1995–96, *24*(1), 55–65.

Ference, P. R., and Vockell, E. L. "Adult Learning Characteristics and Effective Software Instruction." *Educational Technology,* 1994, *34*(6), 25–31.

Gery, G. *Electronic Performance Support Systems: How and Why to Remake the Workplace Through the Strategic Application of Technology.* Boston: Weingarten, 1991.

Gery, G. "Attributes and Behavior of Performance-Centered Systems." *Performance Improvement Quarterly,* 1995a, *8*(1), 47–93.

Gery, G. "EPSS: What It Means for Training." *INFO-LINE At Work,* 1995b, (Winter), 1–2.

Goodrum, D. A., Dorsey, L. T., and Schwen, T. M. "Defining and Building an Enriched Learning and Information Environment." *Educational Technology,* 1993, *33*(11), 10–20.

Hudzina, M., Rowley, K., and Wager, W. "Electronic Performance Support Technology: Defining the Domain." *Performance Improvement Quarterly,* 1996, *9*(1), 36–48.

Kling, R., and Jewett, T. "The Social Design of Worklife with Computers and Networks: A Natural Systems Perspective." In M. Yovitz (ed.), *Advances in Computers* (Vol. 39, pp. 239–293). Orlando: Academic Press, 1994.

Laffey, J. "Dynamism in Electronic Performance Support Systems." *Performance Improvement Quarterly,* 1995, *8*(1), 31–46.

Lave, J., and Wegner, E. *Situated Learning: Legitimate Peripheral Participation.* New York: Cambridge University Press, 1991.

McGraw, K. L. "Performer-Centric Interface Design." *Performance and Instruction,* 1995, *34*(4), 21–29.

McGraw, K. L. "Defining and Designing the Performance-Centered Interface: Moving Beyond the User-Centered Interface." *Interactions: New Visions of Human-Computer Interactions,* 1997, *4*(2), 19–26.

Merriam, S. B. (ed.). *An Update on Adult Learning Theory.* New Directions in Adult and Continuing Education, no. 57. San Francisco: Jossey-Bass, 1993.

Nickerson, R. S. "On the Distribution of Cognition: Some Reflections." In G. Salomon (ed.), *Distributed Cognition: Psychological and Educational Considerations.* New York: Cambridge University Press, 1993.

Norman, D. *Things That Make Us Smart.* Reading, Mass.: Addison-Wesley, 1993.

Pratt, D. D. "Andragogy After Twenty-Five Years." In S. B. Merriam (ed.), *An Update on Adult Learning Theory.* New Directions in Adult and Continuing Education, no. 57. San Francisco: Jossey-Bass, 1993.

Raybould, B. "Performance Support Engineering: An Emerging Development Methodology for Enabling Organizational Learning." *Performance Improvement Quarterly,* 1995, *8*(1), 7–22.

Raybould, B. "The Five Phases of Migration from Training to Knowledge Management." *CBT Solutions,* July/August 1997, pp. 44–47.

Rosenberg, M. J. "Performance Technology, Performance Support, and the Future of Training: A Commentary." *Performance Improvement Quarterly,* 1995, *8*(1), 94–99.

Ryder, M., and Wilson, B. "Affordances and Constraints of the Internet for Learning and Instruction." Paper presented to the Association for Educational Communications and Technology, Indianapolis, Indiana, February 1996.

Salomon, G. "No Distribution Without Individual's Cognition: A Dynamic Interactional View." In G. Salomon (ed.), *Distributed Cognition: Psychological and Educational Considerations.* New York: Cambridge University Press, 1993.

Scales, G., and Yang, C. S. "Perspectives on Electronic Performance Support Systems." Paper presented at the Eastern Educational Research Association Conference, Clearwater, Fla., 1993. (ED 354 883)

Schön, D. A. *The Reflective Practitioner: How Professionals Think in Action.* New York: Basic Books, 1983.

Schwen, T. M., Goodrum, D. A., and Dorsey, L. T. "On the Design of an Enriched Learning and Information Environment (ELIE)." *Educational Technology,* 1993, *33*(11), 5–9.

Sherry, L., and Wilson, B. "Supporting Human Performance Across Disciplines: A Converging of Roles and Tools." *Performance Improvement Quarterly,* 1996, *9*(4), 19–36.

Thomas, B. E., Baron, J. P., and Schmidt, W. J. "Evaluating a Performance Support System for Knowledge Workers" (USACERL Interim Report FF–94/32). Champaign, IL.: Directorate of Military Programs, U.S. Army Corps of Engineers, 1994.

Wilson, A. L. "The Promise of Situated Cognition." In S. B. Merriam (ed.), *An Update on Adult Learning Theory.* New Directions in Adult and Continuing Education, no. 57. San Francisco: Jossey-Bass, 1993.

LINDA S. GILBERT *is currently completing a dissertation in the field of instructional technology and works at the University of Georgia Center for Continuing Education, Athens.*

The World Wide Web offers unique tools for developing on-line instruction. This chapter offers suggestions and guidelines for their effective use.

Course Development on the World Wide Web

Kathleen P. King

It is nine o'clock Monday evening, and Gretchen is logging on to see this week's assignments for her Alternative Teaching Methods course. She checks her e-mail and finds that her professor has suggested some revisions for the draft paper she posted on the class Web site on Friday. Two of her classmates have also e-mailed comments. Gretchen launches her Web browser and opens a bookmark to the class Web site. Options on the home page include "Schedule and Assignments," "Student Projects," "Web Conference," and "Research Resources." Checking the Student Projects page, she sees that Rebecca and Gerry have published drafts of their papers as Web pages, so she skims through them.

At the end of each student paper is a hypertext link that may be used to send e-mail to the author. Gretchen decides to wait to send her comments until she has had time to read the papers more carefully. The asynchronous nature of Web-based interaction benefits Gretchen, whose work schedule prevents her from having as much face-to-face contact with other class members as she would like.

On the Schedule and Assignments page, the professor has assigned a textbook reading on the subject of teaching styles, along with links to a few relevant sites on the Web and to a self-evaluation form. Ready for a break from the computer, Gretchen logs off and curls up on the sofa with her textbook. After finishing the reading, she wants to learn more about her own teaching style and logs on again to complete the self-evaluation. When she clicks the submit button, a Web page showing her results is immediately displayed. Gretchen is tempted to check the Web conference to read what results the other students got, but it's getting late. She'll be able to join the discussion tomorrow, at her convenience. Gretchen feels her contributions to the Web conference are more thoughtful and better appreciated than her comments in the face-to-face class sessions.

Far from being a futuristic scenario, Gretchen's Alternative Teaching Methods class is increasingly typical. Adult students and their teachers are at the forefront of these innovations, using the Web to break down the time and space constraints of a conventional classroom and to experiment with new forms of self-directed and group learning.

This chapter offers adult educators practical advice about using the Web in their courses, providing an overview of the available resources and a set of guidelines for the development of Web-based course materials. While the discussion emphasizes the integration of the Web into traditional face-to-face courses, the same tools and methods can be applied to distance learning as well.

Web Tools for Instruction and Interaction

The Web can be used in many ways in courses, ranging from the simple to the complex (Cyrs, 1997; Fleischman, 1996; Rosen, 1996). Typically, educators begin by using the Web to supplement their courses in basic ways, gradually exploring more complex uses of Web technology. Success may depend on the technical support and computer facilities available to the educator. However, the simplicity and flexibility of the Web make it possible for motivated teachers and trainers to accomplish a great deal, regardless of their prior level of Internet skill.

This chapter does not provide a tutorial on HTML (Hypertext Markup Language) or the other technologies used to create Web pages. However, excellent self-paced tutorials abound, both in print and on the Web (for example, Cearley, 1998; Lemay, 1997; Meyer, 1998). Also, instructors should not underestimate their students as a resource for sharing Web knowledge and participating in the creation of course Web sites.

Starting with Basics. One way to start is to publish a course syllabus as a Web page with a hypertext link allowing students to send e-mail to the teacher. A next step could be a page with a list of links to Web sites on related topics. This list can be compiled through the teacher's research or collaboratively as part of a class assignment. Such a list can include links to search engines, organizations, periodicals, and mailing list archives relevant to the course content. Each time the class is offered, this list should be revised to remove inactive links and add new ones. The development and improvement of such a dynamic resource is a simple but empowering project for adult learners.

Adult learners need to refine their analysis and evaluation skills as they traverse the world of the Web. They will encounter a tremendous amount of information, but just as they have learned to question the messages they receive through traditional media, they must critique Web resources. Instructors can support the development of these skills by assigning students to write short reviews of Web sites and share them with their peers. Having the class contribute to and publish on the Web a list of guidelines or a tutorial about evaluating Web resources would further develop the project; this activity would draw on both their knowledge of paper-based information and their growing experience in navigating the Web.

Advanced Options. Submitting lessons directly to the instructor is one example of a more advanced option that may be included in a Web-supplemented course. This can be done in several ways: via e-mail or FTP (file transfer protocol), or through the class Web site.

E-mail is clearly the simplest strategy. A document can be sent either as the body of an e-mail message or as an attachment to it. Instructors may wish to require the use of plain text files (that is, ASCII format), since translation of word processing documents between different programs and types of computers can be frustrating.

Depending on the availability of technical support, another option may be for students to use fill-in-the-blanks forms on the Web site to submit assignments. Such forms are not difficult to create for those who have learned basic HTML. However, activating them, so that their contents can be stored in a database on the Web server or processed in some other useful way, requires the installation of a CGI (Common Gateway Interface) program on the Web server. CGIs are usually fairly simple programs and many are freely distributed on the Internet (Wright, 1998), but most instructors will need to work closely with their system administrators to implement them.

Adult learners can also take tests through the Web. An on-line test could include multiple choice, true/false, short answer, and essay questions. The results would be sent to the teacher for grading, or in the case of simple objective tests, displayed immediately. Web-based tests require special software; CGIs, JavaScripts (Flanagan, 1997), and Java applets (Niemeyer and Peck, 1997) are all technologies that can support such interactive features. An important caveat about Web-based assessment is that no existing technology can ensure academic honesty. Strategies such as passwords, time limits, and even biometric devices (such as "smart cards" coded to match a handprint) can be subverted by unscrupulous students, unless tests are proctored. Web tests should either be ungraded self-assessments or should be weighed less heavily than the results of monitored exams.

Another popular feature is on-line conferencing. Mailing lists, newsgroups, and Web-based conferencing all support asynchronous dialogues, with students and instructors able to read and contribute messages at any time. Alternatively, synchronous chat programs allow students to experience an immediacy of response similar to face-to-face discussion as they exchange brief text messages in real time. Again, the implementation of on-line conferencing requires technical support from a system administrator.

A variety of software products provide Web server administrators with ready-to-run tools to support testing, conferencing, and other advanced instructional features (see Goldberg and Salari, 1997, for one example of a system that allows instructors to create their own Web courses and tests).

Standardization on such a product at the institutional level can make life much easier for students, faculty, and technical support staff.

Bells and Whistles. The multimedia capabilities of the Web represent a greater level of technical complexity than some of the methods discussed previously, but they provide an exciting indication of features that will become increasingly accessible to teachers and students. Recorded music, voice, and video clips can add great interest and communicative power to a Web site (Horton and Lynch, 1997). However, students need to have appropriate hardware and software to download and hear or view files. This capability is typical of personal computers on the market in 1998, but may be beyond older equipment.

The use of simulated three-dimensional models within a Web site can be especially valuable in science or engineering instruction. For instance, a chemistry Web site can present molecular models that can be rotated and studied from any angle. VRML, Virtual Reality Modeling Language, has emerged as the standard Internet technology for three-dimensional multimedia (VRML Consortium, 1998). Beyond simple modeling, it can also be used for the construction of complex virtual spaces that learners can explore.

All types of multimedia files tend to be large and may take an exorbitant amount of time to download through a modem connection. Therefore, the Web designer should consider the value, format, and size of each multimedia file before including it.

Guidelines for Course Development on the Web

As adult educators begin using the Web to supplement their traditional courses, they must face many questions about technology, curriculum, construction, and evaluation. Each of these areas is discussed in more detail in this section. It may be helpful to create a checklist specific to the institution, class, and instructor that will aid in following through on these questions. It will also be helpful to compile a list of e-mail addresses and phone numbers of people who can serve as resources in each of these areas. The novice Web author should take careful notes during the development process. One cannot rely on memory to recall every detail required in building, administering, and updating a Web site.

Technology. Questions about technology center on the resources of the educational institution and its students. Are Internet access, Web browsers, and other software available, and can a system administrator or technical person be identified who can support the use of these resources? Second, does the institution support student Internet access from off site? If the learners can only use the Web from stations on campus, this will severely limit the amount of time many of them can use it. Third, how many of the learners have other sources of Internet access? If many or all of the students have access from their own computers or through friends, families, public schools, or libraries, it may be possible to work around some institutional limitations. Finally, what are the learners' levels of computer and Internet skills, and what training in these areas is available to them? For some students, mastering the basic skills of Web use might be the extent of one semester's work.

Web course design should be preceded by technological needs assessment. Careful fact-finding in these areas will avoid much frustration later in the process.

Curriculum. Before educators begin lesson plans or Web development, they should review the goals and objectives of their courses and ask how use of the Web can assist in meeting these goals. Technology should assist in meeting clear pedagogical aims, rather than becoming an end in itself. Review of curricular goals leads to the next questions: How will the instructor and students use the Web? What materials will be converted to or created in this format? These questions about course content can only be answered by instructors as subject-matter experts; technical support staff and even instructional designers cannot decide basic curricular issues, though they can often help implement them.

The use of the Web may require a new commitment to andragogical principles (Knowles, 1990). The prior knowledge, self-direction, and orientation to practical application of adult learners are crucial to their ability to master curriculum content within the more flexible class structures enabled by the Web.

Construction. Questions about the construction of the Web site need to be considered next. Who will actually author the Web site? In most cases the teacher will want or need to acquire the skills to do this work directly, relying on Web development software, style guides and books, and workshops or tutorials (Cearley, 1998; Lemay, 1997). In some instances, the instructor may be able to seek technical assistance for all or part of the Web design project. Next, the instructor needs a method to test and evaluate draft versions of the Web pages before the site is made public. This can be done by creating the pages on a personal disk before moving them to a Web server. Third, the teacher needs to determine where the Web site will reside and what the procedures are for transferring files. How easy will it be to make changes to the site? Typically, Web servers are configured so that authorized users can employ FTP to update their Web sites.

Designing the organization of the Web site is best done by sketching a flow chart showing how the pages on the site will be grouped and linked to one another. Careful planning and a clear understanding of Web publishing procedures will allow even inexperienced Web authors to create useful sites in a relatively short period.

Evaluation. A Web site should be evaluated continuously throughout its life cycle. How can it be determined whether or not the site is succeeding in its goals? General criteria may include characteristics such as ease of use, relevance to course topics, and comprehensiveness. Other criteria may center on specific functions of the site, such as assisting in research, fostering student interaction, facilitating feedback on submitted work, promoting critical thinking skills, encouraging reflection, or providing self-assessment tools. Considering these criteria, and above all soliciting detailed feedback from users, will guide the instructor in continually improving the Web site.

How and when will the Web site be evaluated? Learners can fill in on-line comment forms, discuss the usefulness of the site in a Web-based conference, or express their views in person. Students should be encouraged not only to evaluate existing features but also to suggest improvements and new features. Peer review by other faculty and technical evaluation by Web support staff can also be invaluable. Finally, a practical plan for the continued development of the Web site should be established. More than any other communication medium, Web sites have the potential to be changed and improved quickly and globally. A poor Web site is one that is left to stagnate without revisions or updates; planning for continued development from the beginning can over time transform even a very basic Web site into an extremely valuable resource.

Style Guidelines

Several sites on the Web offer detailed style guides that can aid greatly in ensuring ease of use and effectiveness, and can improve consistency for projects involving multiple authors (Horton and Lynch, 1998; Levine, 1995).Some major points are briefly presented here.

- Use white space to improve legibility and comprehension.
- Match the language and design of the site to the skills and needs of its intended audience.
- Keep the course objectives and goals in mind, and omit any material that does not support them.
- Beware of presenting so many links that the focus of the course site is lost.
- Consider the content and layout of Web pages in terms of what will fit on a typical computer screen at one time; long documents are less readable because they require extensive scrolling.
- Organize the Web site so that connections between pages are easy to follow.
- Avoid forcing the user to navigate through too many levels of menus or links to get to frequently needed information.
- Provide readily available navigational buttons or links on every page of the Web site.
- Avoid the use of garish colors, graphics, or animations that reduce the readability of text.
- Encourage feedback by including links for sending e-mail to the designer.

Problems and Pitfalls. As any user of the Web knows, many sites are unattractive and hard to use. Experienced Web authors are also aware of a variety of common hazards that can cost time and cause untold suffering if ignored. Fortunately most of these problems can be circumvented with a little planning.

- Check links to external pages often, and change or remove them when they become invalid.

- Beware of the potential difficulties in moving an entire site to another Web server; links within the site may have to be changed. Use relative rather than absolute links to avoid this problem.
- When giving demonstrations or presentations of the site, be sure to have an alternate means of access, or, better, a copy of the site on disk, in case of network failures.
- Be aware that some students have little, if any, computer or Web experience; try to give simple explanations without unnecessary technical jargon.
- Do not depend on one person to make all the site changes and updates.
- Make frequent backups of the course Web site and store them in safe locations.

Conclusion

Web-based courses can offer learners increased independence, greater productivity, and new experiences. Even in institutional settings where educators do not yet have the resources or support to build Web sites, it may be possible to prepare the way with field trips to a computer lab. Demonstration and practice are much more effective in conveying the value of the Web than handwaving and flow charts on a chalk board. Instructors can help even resistant adult learners begin to use the Web by providing the addresses of relevant sites in class, including them in reference lists, and, once resources are available, beginning to build a Web site with them. A course Web site can remain a vital resource for adult learners long after they have completed the course. Web-based courses provide an opportunity to empower students to reach beyond their individual experience and to see the activity of learning as something that extends beyond the classroom.

A Web site does not have to be done all at once; in the words of one experienced developer, "The paint never dries." Even a simple one-page site can be expanded and improved over time. Asking oneself the questions about technology, curriculum, construction, and evaluation posed in this chapter can simplify that process, and adherence to a style guide can make your site more attractive and easier to use.

The tremendous growth of the Web over the last few years reflects the fact that technologies like HTML and HTTP have made it possible for nontechnical people to learn to share their knowledge on the Internet. By acquiring basic Web development skills, and by empowering students to use the Web, instructors can help enable new patterns of adult learning that will long outlive the current generation of Web technology.

References

Cearley, K. *HTML 4 Interactive Course.* Corte Madera, Calif.: Waite Group Press, 1998.
Cyrs, T. E. (ed.). *Teaching and Learning at a Distance: What It Takes to Effectively Design, Deliver, and Evaluate Programs.* New Directions for Teaching and Learning, no. 71. San Francisco: Jossey-Bass, 1997.

Flanagan, D. *JavaScript: The Definitive Guide*. (2nd ed.) Sebastopol, Calif.: O'Reilly & Associates, 1997.

Fleischman, J. "The Web: New Venue for Adult Education." *Adult Learning*, 1996, 8(1), 17–18.

Goldberg, M. W., and Salari, S. "An Update on WebCT (World-Wide Web Course Tools): A Tool for the Creation of Web-Based Learning Environments." [http://homebrew.cs.ubc.ca/Webct/papers/nauWeb/full-paper.html]. June, 1997.

Horton, S., and Lynch, P. L. "Web Multimedia: Turning the Corner." *Syllabus*, 1997, 4(11), 16, 18, 20.

Horton, S., and Lynch, P. L. "Yale Center for Advanced Instructional Media Web Style Guide." [http://info.med.yale.edu/caim/manual/index.html]. Mar. 1998.

Knowles, M. S. *The Adult Learner: A Neglected Species*. (4th ed.) Houston: Gulf, 1990.

Lemay, L. *Teach Yourself Web Publishing with HTML in a Week*. (4th ed.) Indianapolis, Ind.: Samsnet, 1997.

Levine, R. "Guide to Web Style." [http://www.sun.com/styleguide/]. Aug. 1996.

Meyer, E. A. "Introduction to HTML." [http://www.cwru.edu/help/introHTML/toc.html]. Mar. 1998.

Niemeyer, P., and Peck, J. *Exploring Java*. (2nd ed.) Sebastopol, Calif.: O'Reilly & Associates, 1997.

Rosen, D. J. "Learning to Ride the Web: How Adult Students and Teachers Are 'Surfing' the Internet." *Adult Learning*, 1996, 8(1), 15–16.

VRML Consortium. "The Virtual Reality Modeling Language Consortium." [http://www.vrml.org/]. Mar. 1998.

Wright, M. "CGI Resource Index" [http://www.cgi-resources.com/]. Mar. 1998.

KATHLEEN P. KING is assistant professor and program coordinator of adult education at Fordham University, Graduate School of Education, New York, New York.

Adults use the Internet to achieve different kinds of learning through different types of educational experiences. This chapter describes research on adult students in Internet-based courses and ways to enhance their learning.

Adult Learners and Internet-Based Distance Education

Daniel V. Eastmond

As society moves from an industrial to an information base, adults are rapidly becoming involved in using the Internet for professional, personal, and educational purposes. Over half of the full-time workforce in the United States uses computers regularly in their jobs (DiNardo and Pischke, 1997), and increasingly these computers are networked. More than 35 percent of households own a computer (Negroponte, 1995), and these are quickly being connected to the Internet as adults and children use the World Wide Web for information, entertainment, and education. Rapidly changing societal and work environments demand continuous learning, and nontraditional students (over twenty-five, part-time, working, residing off campus) are the new majority, pursuing education for career development, job security, upward mobility, recareering, and other professional and personal reasons.

Distance education (defined as a separation of teachers and students interacting through mediated technologies under the auspices of an institution) is becoming widely accepted as a means for higher education to provide broader access and achieve cost-efficiencies while maintaining quality programs. A dozen or more *virtual institutions* have emerged, offering or brokering college courses for adults while providing important administrative and academic supports, often without a physical campus of their own.

A Typology of Internet Uses in Distance Education

Distance education providers are faced with the challenge of moving their adult students, faculty, advisers, and courses from the traditional low-tech delivery technologies of print, telephone, and mail to Internet technologies such as

New Directions for Adult and Continuing Education, no. 78, Summer 1998 © Jossey-Bass Publishers

e-mail and the Web. These high-tech environments are less familiar to most adults, requiring some skill with computers, and challenge educators to rethink their instructional approaches. Eastmond and Granger (1997) present a three-tiered typology for courses using Internet technology that provides a framework for distance institutions to progress along a continuum from lesser to greater technological sophistication. This flexible typology can be applied to various configurations of traditional and nontraditional delivery methods to aid educators in planning and implementing Internet-based education.

Depending on the type of Internet technology a distance course employs, adults will tend to learn differently. Concluding their review of adult learning theories, Merriam and Caffarella (1991) found that adult learning tends to be self-directed, that life experiences trigger and aid adult learning, and that reflection and action are integral components of the adult learning process. Other educators of adults characterize successful learning as including additional attributes such as collaboration, interactivity, application, democracy, constructivism, and a sense of community. Whatever the Internet activity, students must learn how to learn in these new instructional environments, and educators must recognize how different aspects of technology influence different characteristics of adult learning. The following descriptions of technology types indicate some of these connections.

Type I: Traditional Distance Learning Supplemented with Internet Activities. Beginning the continuum are courses that are primarily delivered through another distance means (for example, telephone-supported correspondence study) but that incorporate Internet-based activities and assignments. Typically these allow students to participate in e-mail exchanges with instructors and other students; support on-line research in libraries, databases, electronic journals, and Web sites; and may also make use of on-line discussion groups such as mailing lists, newsgroups, Web-based conferences, and real-time (synchronous) chat. Since the Internet is not the primary delivery medium for a Type I course, adult learners can venture into computer telecommunications in a low-risk way, knowing that these skills will be valuable in the future.

Type I courses can foster self-direction by allowing students to choose assignments that fit their professional needs or developmental tasks and to select Internet resources to address them. A student explains: "What I've found is that this form of education online gets you into experiential learning . . . [the professor] gives you objectives for the course . . . and a guidebook on how to get into the system and all the mentoring help that you need . . . and then it is up to you . . . to discover. What a way to learn! When I got into this telecommunications I began to see myself how well we learn from doing" (Eastmond, 1995, p. 82).

On-line activities can engender experiential learning most effectively when they are placed within a context of previous experience and when adults try out new technologies for communication and research. As another student noted, "[Two other class members] and I have a project to do for Monday. This [e-mail discussion] is a good way to coordinate it. I can get a message direct from a classmate rather than try to decipher a phone message note, and it is cheaper than calling. What a deal" (Yakimovicz and Murphy, 1995, p. 205).

Unlike television, which often places adults in the position of passive recipients, Internet activities require active learning—taking responsibility and accepting new experiences as opportunities for growth (Cook, 1995).

Type II: Computer Conferencing. Although students still use a printed course guide and textbooks and exchange assignments through the mail, in the Type II course the Internet becomes the main vehicle of instruction and communication. The conversational environment is usually a text-only computer conference with topical *threads* (sequences of messages), although mailing lists are sometimes used. On-line discussions are usually *asynchronous* (that is, participants are not accessing and contributing to the conversation at the same time). This type of course requires more interaction with other students, and students must learn to pace themselves to keep up with course communications. Students who are used to other distance or classroom delivery formats must adjust to not being able to see or hear their instructor or other students.

What kind of adult learning does computer conferencing foster? Beyond the experiential and activity learning characteristic of Type I, there is a great emphasis on interactivity—receiving in-depth, meaningful feedback to one's contributions from peers as well as the instructor, and the ability to respond in return. Type II Internet courses also require more reflection, as students consider how new information and experiences fit within the context of prior knowledge. One adult learner explained, "Many times I have needed to digest and reflect on information given in a class presentation and have not been able to intelligently comment or ask questions on the spot. The [mailing list] has provided a sense of delay in terms of synthesizing the data presented, and yet everyone still gets informed of what you are thinking" (Yakimovicz and Murphy, 1995, p. 208).

Additionally, on-line class discussions allow adult learners to collaborate, working together in creating an assignment or performing a task in which the joint outcome is more complex than it could have been if done individually. A student in a Type II course described the support of peers in a group writing effort this way: "[One man] took the time to respond to everybody's writing, not just in his small group. He was very supportive and encouraging. . . . [It was intimidating] knowing that your peers were going to critique [your work]. And then as we got into it, myself in particular, as I saw the quality of the writing of the other people, it was even more intimidating, and yet they were so encouraging that you also wanted to just keep improving on your work. It was delightful" (Eastmond, 1995, pp. 138–140).

Type III: Virtual Courses and Institutions. The third type of technology on this continuum leads to Web-based courses offered by a virtual institution. A Web-based course can extend the textual resources characteristic of Type II with colorful graphics, audio and video segments, and hypertext links.

These courses may include off-line activities (such as conducting interviews, reading a textbook, going on site visits, or observing a cultural event or lecture), but most aspects of the course are on-line: the course guide, the electronic discussions with the instructor and other students, the links to Web resources that support the course content and on-line activities, and the submission and return of assignments.

The Web-based interface can facilitate students' interactions with the institution for a full range of on-line academic and administrative services, from course registration and book ordering to reviewing academic records and receiving counseling. Type III technology requires the highest levels of computer equipment and sophistication of user skills, not only for students but for instructors, advisers, administrators, and support staff.

Courses based on Type III technology, involving a deeper immersion in the Web environment, can promote constructivist learning and foster virtual learning communities. Yakimovicz and Murphy (1995) report that participants in electronic discussion groups found that effective communication was a socially constructed behavior, as groups formed and discovered their own participation norms. Learners struggled to comprehend the perspective of others as they created their own meanings: "It is difficult reading some [Internet] messages. I have to try and figure out the perspective of someone I have never met, never seen, and most likely have never shared a similar environment with" (Yakimovicz and Murphy, 1995, p. 206).

Unlike a traditional neighborhood that is defined by geographical proximity, today adults can be involved in multiple Internet communities, composed of "students, experts, and learning facilities from around the world" (Cook, 1995, p. 36). These communities can be more democratic than traditional ones because asynchronous on-line discussion gives all participants the ability to compose and contribute messages that are as lengthy as they please. Near the end of an on-line course, one student expressed the sense of community in these terms: "A lot of [the class members'] closing thoughts were how wonderful it was to use the computer because they were no longer alone. They felt the connection with other students, and they liked being able to talk back and forth and get different perspectives" (Eastmond, 1995, p. 17).

Studies about Adult Learning with On-Line Instruction

Research on student experiences with Internet-based distance education indicates that it is living up to its educational promise. Several studies are representative of the levels of the typology described in the previous section.

A Study of Type I Technology. Yakimovicz and Murphy (1995) conducted a qualitative study of the Internet experience of a graduate class of adult students delivered through interactive video and audio conferencing supported by computer-mediated communications. As part of the course requirements, students were required to exchange e-mail with class members, subscribe to an electronic newsletter, and participate in a classwide discussion group as well as in a larger mailing list that connected students and faculty at eight institutions in the United States and Australia.

The report on this Type I course states that students progressed from process management concerns (that is, learning to use the technology for learning) to *meaning-making* (that is, constructing new knowledge within their personal knowledge structures). These adult graduate students worked together to overcome technical difficulties and supported each other in learning to use the Internet activities of the course. They adjusted their communication styles to deal with tangential conversations, to converse with unknown persons, and to time their contributions so that they would be effective.

The authors suggest that students gained a new sense of themselves through the Internet activities of the course, as their opinions were affirmed by others who responded to their messages and they became confident of their abilities to work and learn on-line. These adults constructed new meanings for the nature of computer-mediated communication and the Internet, and became excited about the new world they had discovered in cyberspace.

Studies of Type II Technology. Several qualitative studies have examined the student experience in Type II (computer conferencing) courses in depth (Burge, 1994; Eastmond, 1995; Harasim, 1987). Some of the elements adult students liked about these courses were asynchronicity (accessing the course as it fit their schedule), group support (feeling camaraderie in their new learning experience), reflection (considering their words carefully before responding), control (feeling independent about studying), interactivity (giving and receiving feedback about on-line messages), text (engaging in intensive reading and writing activities), and democracy (feeling that each participant had equitable "air time").

However, these elements are not inherent in the technology but must be fostered by course design, instructor engagement, and student behavior. Eastmond (1995) reported that students experienced little interactivity when they didn't keep up with or contribute actively to discussions. Asynchronicity became a challenge as students tried to keep pace with each other's contributions. Although some participants seriously reflected in composing their responses, most participants replied informally and spontaneously. Finally, on-line groups were not supportive of all participants, and discussions sometimes became more competitive than collaborative.

Learning orientation largely determined the extent to which adult students found the computer conferencing activity important. Those who saw learning as a means of mastering an external body of knowledge found the on-line course less important than those whose aim in learning was to construct personal meaning through interaction with course content and their peers (Eastmond, 1995). Although students used many of the strategies noted in taxonomies of learning (for example, managing one's student role and the learning environment, learning individually and in groups, thinking creatively and practically, and applying problem-solving techniques for making decisions), Burge (1994) found that it was also necessary for students to develop strategies for managing peer behavior and meta-context.

Although students transferred learning approaches from other delivery formats to this Type II course, they developed unique responses to learning the technology, deciding participation frequency, dealing with information overload, handling textual ambiguity, processing on-line information, and determining how to respond. Students in on-line courses learned these strategies incidentally and placed little value on their importance, but in fact such informal learning appeared to play an important role in their success in the courses (Eastmond, 1995).

A Study of Type III Technology. Students of the SUNY Learning Network (SLN) may be typical of those interacting with Type III courses at a virtual college (in this case, a consortium of participating SUNY institutions). The SLN (accessible at http://www.sln.suny.edu/sln/) provides over a hundred courses from more than twenty SUNY institutions via the Web, sharing some common administrative support such as a course management system, a help desk (available on-line and by 800 telephone number), and an enrollment system. Credit and degrees are offered by the host institutions.

During the Spring 1997 term, a third of the 108 students enrolled in SLN courses through Empire State College responded to three on-line surveys (Eastmond, 1997). This was the first distance course for 56 percent of the respondents. They were taking the course for educational reasons (37 percent), out of personal interest (26 percent), to develop job skills or knowledge (23 percent), or to learn about computer network technology (15 percent).

Students averaged five hours of coursework a week on-line and ten hours off-line. About half thought the workload was comparable to other college courses, but 39 percent thought it was greater. Seventy-nine percent reported having supportive home and work environments. Their comments reveal challenges similar to those adult students often face: having professional or personal tasks take precedence over course participation; struggling to find space and time for school work; coping with family annoyance at having the telephone line tied up for network connections; and needing to take distance courses because of employment constraints.

With each successive survey, students increasingly saw on-line conversations with other students as contributing to their learning. They liked hearing from all students, not just the most vocal ones; having the freedom to express themselves in an environment of partial anonymity; and learning from students with a wide range of pertinent experiences and opinions. However, some found these conversations time-consuming, disjointed, time-delayed, and intimidating. Respondents valued interactions with instructors (63 percent at midterm, 71 percent at course-end), particularly when they responded quickly, kept the class discussion on track, and were readily available for individual attention.

Major obstacles reported were the technology itself (30 percent), demanding study schedules (28 percent), and difficult content (13 percent). Major benefits were flexibility of time and location (26 percent), interesting content (20 percent), and an enhanced learning environment (17 percent). Most students reported good or excellent tutor performance (80 percent) and administrative support (77 percent), and wanted to take more Web-based courses in the future.

Adult Learner Progress in Internet Courses

Many of the findings about student success in completing traditional distance education programs are also applicable to Internet-based courses. In comprehensive research on factors that lead to student persistence, Kember (1995) found that social and academic integration play critical roles in adult distance study success. Successful learners become socially integrated by negotiating support for their study time and resources from their employer, coworkers, family, and friends, and they take direct control and responsibility for their distance studies, working within the norms of the institution. Students become integrated academically in their distance study when they feel affiliation with the institution, share the same expectations about academic performance as faculty, take a deep approach to learning (see next paragraph), are intrinsically motivated, receive positive evaluations, and read with enjoyment and breadth. Kember (1995) outlines how distance institutions can facilitate integration by providing stronger course design, teaching, counseling, orientation, and administrative support services.

Instructional designers can foster adult success in Internet courses by incorporating activities that promote the dimensions of adult learning mentioned earlier (Eastmond and Ziegahn, 1995). Additionally, they can individualize activities and assignments. Course guides should suggest strategies for learning with on-line environments and resources. Finally, courses should be designed to foster a *deep learning* approach, in which students find enjoyment and meaning in a personalized academic task that fits into a holistic view of the subject while eschewing *surface learning*, which is caused by excessively heavy workload, shallow assessment, extrinsic interest, and a lack of freedom in activities and assignments (Kember, 1995).

Supportive on-line teaching demands that faculty actively guide the on-line discourse in a caring, stimulating manner (Eastmond, 1992; Harasim, 1991; Rohfeld and Hiemstra, 1995). On-line instructors can use a variety of techniques to enliven courses, such as small group discussions, role-playing, student presentations, brainstorming, and simulations. Effective teachers give individual attention in private messages and provide summarizing comments in the general discussion to keep the conversation on course.

The virtual institution also needs to provide academic and administrative services via the Internet to help create a sense of integration for adult learners as they progress through distance degree programs. These on-line facilities can include advisement and counseling; assessment of prior learning; on-line academic resources; book purchasing and delivery; a help center for technical, academic, and administrative concerns; career development; and admission, registration, and academic record services.

Conclusion

Distance education has expanded to the Internet to the extent that in some settings the terms *distance learning* and *Web-based courses* are becoming synonymous. This learning environment provides tremendous convenience and flexibility, allowing busy, mobile adult learners to engage in education when and where they wish. Beyond its logistical advantages, the Internet holds important educational promise for engendering active and experiential learning, encouraging reflection and application, and fostering collaboration and individualized construction of meaning in learning communities that extend beyond the boundaries of the traditional classroom or campus. However, faculty, staff, administrators, institutions, and students face many challenges in taking full advantage of these learning environments. The typology presented in this chapter can help educators understand the different levels at which Internet technologies can support adult learning.

Research about Internet-based instruction indicates generally positive student response and desire for more courses of the same type. Although initial institutional efforts at Internet-based distance learning tend to be directed toward course design and faculty training, the fully established Internet institution will have to provide a broad range of academic and administrative support if it is to establish and sustain successful adult learning.

References

Burge, E. J. "Learning in Computer Conference Contexts: The Learner's Perspective." *Journal of Distance Education,* 1994, *9*(1), 19–43.

Cook, D. L. "Community and Computer-Generated Distance Learning Environments." In M. H. Rossman and M. E. Rossman (eds.), *Facilitating Distance Education.* New Directions in Adult and Continuing Education, no. 67. San Francisco: Jossey-Bass, 1995.

DiNardo, J. E., and Pischke, J. S. "The Returns to Computer Use Revisited: Have Pencils Changed the Wage Structure Too?" *Quarterly Journal of Economics,* 1997, *112*(1), 291–303.

Eastmond, D. V. "Effective Facilitation of Computer Conferencing." *Continuing Higher Education Review,* 1992, *56*(1 and 2), 23–34.

Eastmond, D. V. *Alone But Together: Adult Distance Study by Computer Conferencing.* Cresskill, N.J.: Hampton Press, 1995.

Eastmond, D. V. "Results of Surveys of Students in Empire State College's SUNY Learning Network Courses." Unpublished memorandum. Center for Distance Learning, SUNY Empire State College, 1997.

Eastmond, D. V., and Granger, D. "Reaching Distance Students Through Computer Network Technology." *Distance Education Report,* 1997, *1*(2, 3, and 4), 4–6, 4–6, 4–6.

Eastmond, D. V., and Ziegahn, L. "Instructional Design and the Online Classroom." In Z. Berge and M. P. Collins (eds.), *Computer-Mediated Communications and the Online Classroom,* Vol. III: Distance Learning. Cresskill, N.J.: Hampton Press, 1995.

Harasim, L. M. "Teaching and Learning On-Line: Issues in Computer-Mediated Graduate Courses." *Canadian Journal of Educational Communication,* 1987, *16*(2), 117–135.

Harasim, L. M. "Teaching by Computer Conferencing." In A. Miller (ed.), *Applications of Computer Conferencing to Teacher Education and Human Resource Development: Proceedings of the International Symposium on Computer Conferencing.* Columbus: Ohio State University, 1991.

Kember, D. *Open Learning Courses for Adults: A Model of Student Progress.* Englewood Cliffs, N.J.: Educational Technology Publications, 1995.

Merriam, S. B., and Caffarella, R. S. *Learning in Adulthood: A Comprehensive Guide.* San Francisco: Jossey-Bass, 1991.

Negroponte, N. P. *Being Digital.* New York: Vintage Books, 1995.

Rohfeld, R. W., and Hiemstra, R. "Moderating Discussions in the Electronic Classroom." In Z. Berge and M. P. Collins (eds.), *Computer-Mediated Communications and the Online Classroom,* Vol. III: Distance Learning. Cresskill, N.J.: Hampton Press, 1995.

Yakimovicz, A. D., and Murphy, K. L. "Constructivism and Collaboration on the Internet: Case Study of a Graduate Class Experience." *Computers and Education,* 1995, 24(3), 203–209.

DANIEL V. EASTMOND is assistant professor of technology for training and development, School of Education, University of South Dakota, Vermillion.

A series of Internet-based National Issues Forums illuminates challenges for facilitators of on-line discussions and pitfalls and possibilities for group learning of critical thinking skills.

Facilitating Group Learning on the Internet

Margaret E. Holt, Pamela B. Kleiber, Jill Dianne Swenson, E. Frances Rees, Judy Milton

The Internet offers an unprecedented environment for experimentation in collaborative learning, expanding beyond teacher-student interactions to synergistic explorations by diverse groups. This chapter summarizes research conducted from 1994 to 1996 using electronic mailing lists and Web-based conferencing with the goal of developing a better understanding of the nature of electronically facilitated study groups.

Background

The participants were students from "Issues and the News" journalism classes at Ithaca College and adult education classes in "Methods" and "Public Policy" at the University of Georgia, who took part in a series of on-line National Issues Forums.

National Issues Forums were introduced in the United States in 1981 by the Charles F. Kettering Foundation and the Public Agenda Foundation (Holt, Rees, Swenson, and Kleiber, 1997). Each year these foundations and other partners develop nonpartisan discussion materials on public policy issues, framed around three or four choices for consideration and potential action. These forums are designed to help citizens develop the discursive and reflective skills necessary for effective participation in democratic debate and decision making. Participation has increased dramatically each year, and forums are conducted in a variety of settings, including colleges and universities, civic organizations, libraries, and prisons. Until recently, forums were almost entirely face-to-face exchanges. This research was a series of efforts to extend the

National Issues Forum model to the Internet, to study its effectiveness there, and to evolve new methods of facilitation for the on-line environment.

In 1994, students in Athens, Georgia, and Ithaca, New York, discussed "People and Politics," in 1995 "Affirmative Action," and in 1996 "How Should We Govern America?" During the first two years, the forums were conducted through mailing lists; the third-year forum used a Web-based conferencing program, Facilitate.com (McCall and Szerdy, 1998).

Each of the three forums lasted for six weeks. Management and facilitation procedures were based on those developed for previous National Issues Forums, modified for the electronic context. Every week two collaborating moderators posted a topic, posing several options in question format, and invited participant responses. A moderator at each site provided technical support for the student participants, while the on-line moderators took responsibility for facilitating the deliberative dialogues. Before each forum began, participants were provided guidelines for on-line discussion, including *netiquette* (etiquette for the Internet), and signed informed consent and research statements. "The Electronic Forum Handbook: Study Circles in Cyberspace" (Kleiber, Holt, and Swenson, 1996), based upon the initial mailing list experience in 1994, guided the process during the 1995 and 1996 forums.

Research Concepts, Questions, and Methods

Computer-mediated communication is increasingly seen as a powerful tool for collaborative learning and teaching, but research evaluating such efforts is still sparse, and opinions are divided on their effectiveness. Collaborative technology, it is argued, supports "mutual knowledge construction" by allowing participants to create "shared resolutions" to ill-defined problems (Roschelle, 1992), while offering opportunities for broader participation, more dynamic interaction, and the creation of a sense of virtual community. However, some have suggested that existing research has failed to pose the right questions, emphasizing comparisons to face-to-face learning without sufficient focus on the actual quality and meaning of distance learning for the participants.

Ehrmann (1995) reflects a not-uncommon ambivalence about the practical value of computer-mediated communication: "I've got two pieces of bad news about that experimental English comp course where students used computer conferencing. First, over the course of the semester, the experimental group showed no progress in abilities to compose an essay. The second piece of bad news is that the control group, taught by traditional methods, showed no progress either" (p. 20). Shaffer and Anundsen (1993) express greater optimism: "Used with wisdom and compassion, computer networks help people adapt to the sometimes frightening new world that technology itself has helped to create. Ignoring electronic technology can be as much a hazard as misusing it; those who cannot adapt to the computer's pervasive presence will eventually isolate themselves. It is essential to stay alert to both the dangers and the incredible opportunities that networks present—to use technology to build real solidarity" (p. 148). One goal of this research was to put both the ambivalence and the optimism surrounding computer-mediated learning to a series of practical tests.

The type of learning investigated in this research emphasized critical and reflective thinking, specifically the skills necessary for "deliberation" as operationally defined in the development of the forums over several years. The literature on critical and reflective thinking is primarily concerned with the individual thought process (King and Kitchener, 1994). This project concentrated on public deliberation as a process in which individuals develop the knowledge and skills to think collaboratively within a forum designed to consider ill-structured, emotionally powerful problems.

In their analysis of the development of critical thinking in distance learning, Anderson and Garrison (1995) discuss the importance of a community of inquiry, citing interaction between and among students and teachers as necessary to meaningful learning. Entwistle and Entwistle (1991), in a study with undergraduates, found that the negotiation of shared meaning emerged as one of the main strategies used to ensure understanding. Through conversation and, ultimately, critical discourse, higher-order thinking skills develop in formal education as well as through individual learning endeavors.

The National Issues Forums have focused since 1981 on the public deliberative process through which people articulate their own perspectives and opinions and listen to the perspectives and opinions of others in an effort to weigh choices. In this sense, deliberation is akin to what King and Kitchener (1994) describe as reflective judgment.

There were three major research questions about this form of group learning:

- Does deliberation occur on-line?
- Can a deliberative process be learned through participation in an electronic forum?
- Do on-line forums contribute to the development of deliberative skills?

A tremendous advantage in researching the nature of learning electronically is that the full text of on-line discussions can be preserved and analyzed. For each of the three forums, the corpus of student postings was subjected to discourse analysis both during and after the forum. Additional sources of data included both on-line and off-line evaluations conducted using summative questionnaires and student journals.

Selected Findings

Deliberation. Through protocol and discourse analysis, the research identified stages of deliberation occurring over the course of the forums. The stages were formalized in a six-step model of public deliberation that included two stages of pre-deliberation, two stages of quasi-deliberation, and two stages of deliberation. These findings were largely consistent with the theoretical literature about critical and reflective thinking, small group theory, cognitive development, and participatory democracy (Abramson, 1994; Brookfield, 1987; Ennis and Millman, 1971; Fishkin, 1991, 1995; Gastil, 1994, 1995; Gastil, Adams, and Jenkins-Smith, 1995; Halpern, 1996; Hustedde, 1996; King and Kitchener, 1994; Kohlberg, 1984; Mathews, 1994; McKenzie, 1996; Mishoe, 1994; Paul, 1990; Perry, 1970; Piaget, 1974; Pratkanis and Turner, 1996; Watson and Glaser, 1964; Yankelovich, 1991).

In the first pre-deliberative stage, participants began to build common ground by learning about a pressing public issue and sharing their personal interests, beliefs, and values, tending to use first-person language and declarative, assertive syntax. The second pre-deliberative stage saw participants staking out personal opinions, and conversation was increasingly couched in terms of "you and me" and "us and them." The third stage was quasi-deliberative, as the group began to weigh the advantages and disadvantages of various perspectives; premature consensus was a risk here. The fourth stage showed an increasing focus on the public good, revolving around consequences, outcomes, and implications of the choices facing the group. By this point language had become more objective, with a stronger use of the plural *we* and possessive *our*. The fifth stage was group decision making or public judgment; without forcing consensus, participants made individual choices premised on rational grounds. The sixth and final stage turned to the possibilities of public action based on these judgments, with language returning to the first person as participants articulated "what I can do" as a member of the community.

This model of the stages of deliberation reflects the cumulative results of the three forums. Discourse analysis of the first mailing list forum indicated little evidence of public deliberation. This discrepancy is a finding worthy of more detailed discussion.

Differences Between Mailing List and Web-Based Forums. In the mailing lists, participants tended to interact individually with the moderators, but very little with one another independent of the moderators. Several reported frustration when they e-mailed a comment or question and received no replies. One said, "I need immediate feedback, which allows for clarification of content and follow-up questions or comments." This and similar feedback alerted the forum organizers to the importance of not allowing words to hang unanswered in cyberspace, thereby creating and intensifying isolation. Another participant commented, "I was a little disappointed in not knowing how most felt about what I was sending. I could not know who agreed or disagreed with my comments except those who stated so." Overflowing mailboxes but little continuity between messages created an impression of disconnection and hindered true deliberation.

In contrast, following a topic on the Web was clearly easier for participants, because of the more coherent visual sequencing of ideas. On the mailing lists, it was necessary for facilitators and participants to sift through large numbers of messages that arrived out of order. On the Web, all postings on a topic appeared as part of a single document. Each reloading of this Web page sorted postings and their appended comments so that the ones with the most recent comments appeared first, which tended to shift less relevant postings downward on the page while keeping the areas of greatest common interest near the top. Students reported themselves able to participate more efficiently when using this Web interface, and orientation sessions by instructors took much less time.

Data suggest that participant reflection may be greater in a Web conference because of the ability to reread an entire sequence of postings while composing a response. The Web format also appears to encourage participants to take more responsibility for their choices by making it easier for the group to stay on topic; when a participant goes off topic, the effect is more obvious than it is among a welter of e-mail, and the group either calls attention to it or ignores it. The structure of Web conferencing also makes it possible for moderators and others to intervene with critical questions at the point of reference, rather than in a detached message.

Caution is warranted in drawing broader conclusions from these differences, because successive cohorts of students no doubt brought greater familiarity with Internet technologies to each year of the forum, but participant feedback and productivity clearly indicated the superiority of Web-based conferencing for the purpose of the National Issues Forums.

Persona of the Moderator. The responsibilities of the on-line moderator seem to be determined more by the purpose of the group than by the medium. The National Issues Forums have clearly stated purposes and a well-defined structure for achieving them. When forum participants take responsibility for their own deliberative work, the moderator remains in the background, but the silent presence of the moderator helps provide a sense of order. A moderator who does need to become involved in the process is most effective when speaking in the voice of a neutral, third-party persona, and not in the personal voice of the individual. This helps to ensure that even when the moderator takes an active or proactive role in a forum, interaction remains centered on the issues rather than personalities.

Assessing Individual Learning. Deliberation can be measured by looking at the patterns of engagement of the participants. Within the context of National Issues Forums, the deliberative process is used to teach experientially a particular way of reasoning and talking together that requires the use of critical and reflective skills as participants engage a broad range of choices, weigh their pros and cons, and come to judgment about common concerns. The quantity and quality of participant-to-participant exchanges is thus an index of individual learning.

For some participants, critical thinking abilities evolved over the course of the forums, especially the ability to reflect. Asked if the Web conference encouraged communication, one student replied, "I began to see communication as a real effort to facilitate change and believe in the importance of a collective voice. I started to ponder issues and talk with friends about them."

Another said, "Socially, I appreciated hearing the others' opinions and greatly appreciated the icebreakers. I felt somewhat intimidated by the subject and therefore took awhile in warming up . . . I wanted to at least make some intelligent remarks that were accurate."

Students in both mailing list and Web forums reported effects on their reflective thinking that extended beyond the activity itself. They appreciated being asked what they thought about the issues, observed it was necessary to ponder the questions before responding, and said the process prohibited automatic reactions. One student reported, "Most of the time my best responses came after I exited the forum." Another said, "I learned by analyzing others' opinions, the questions proposed and by evaluating my own beliefs and feelings."

Challenges for Facilitators. Groups are difficult and complex in face-to-face experiences and even more so in on-line forums where a clear sense of personal presence is difficult to sustain. Many of the cues that govern ordinary social interaction are absent: eye contact, body language, facial expressions, and voice tone, for example. Facilitators must find ways to mitigate the effects of these differences.

Facilitating on-line learning involves many responsibilities: creating the environment, guiding the process, providing points of departure, moderating the process, managing the content, and creating community. Strategies for creating a sense of community include establishing ground rules and expectations, using introductions and icebreakers, suggesting ways for connecting participants off-line, and involving participants directly in the process of community creation by inviting their ideas on ways to make this happen.

In many cases, the same aspects of on-line conferencing that were its greatest benefits for participants formed its most difficult challenges for facilitators (Holt, Milton, and McCall, 1998). Table 5.1 summarizes some of these parallel benefits and challenges.

Conclusion

Clearly there were many limitations to these early studies, including short time frames, hardware and software problems, mandatory rather than self-selected participation, difficulties of access to computers, differences in individual computer skills, and differences in commitment to the process. The research partially answered some questions and generated many more.

Further research is needed to investigate the structuring and sequencing of electronic forums, strategies for combining face-to-face and electronic experiences, techniques for effective moderation of on-line conferences, and methods of modeling critical thinking skills in on-line environments. In particular, longitudinal studies focusing on the sustainability of on-line communities could advance our understanding of their value for lifelong learning.

Table 5.1. Benefits and Challenges of Using Web Conferencing

Benefits for Participants	Challenges for Moderators and Facilitators
More people can participate without restraints of time and place.	Participants must have access to tools and the skills to use them.
People who may not be comfortable participating in face-to-face groups have a voice.	Silent ("lurking") participants remain invisible to the group.
Asynchronous communication allows flexibility in individual schedules.	Participants must be encouraged to schedule and spend time on the process.
Participants have time and space to focus independently on the process and content.	Loss of face-to-face social interaction affects development of group identity.
Participants have time for reflection rather than knee-jerk reactions.	Participants need responsive feedback to avoid feelings of isolation.
More data and ideas are collected.	Coping with the volume of data generated can be overwhelming.
Participants have unlimited space to express their views.	Participants must be encouraged to keep messages concise and on-topic.
Everyone can see everyone else's contributions and build upon them.	The moderator must help funnel ideas and discussion to achieve decisions.
Satisfaction with the process produces increased buy-in to results.	Resistance may be difficult to perceive and engage.

References

Abramson, J. We, the Jury: The Jury System and the Ideal of Democracy. New York: Basic Books, 1994.

Anderson, T. D., and Garrison, D. R. "Critical Thinking in Distance Education: Developing Critical Communities in an Audio Teleconferences Context." Higher Education, 1995, 29, 183–199.

Brookfield, S. Developing Critical Thinkers: Challenging Adults to Explore Alternative Ways of Thinking and Acting. San Francisco: Jossey-Bass, 1987.

Ehrmann, S. C. "Asking the Right Questions: What Does Research Tell Us About Technology and Higher Learning?" Change, 1995, 27(2), 20–27.

Ennis, R. H., and Millman, J. Cornell Critical Thinking Test. Urbana, Ill.: Critical Thinking Project, University of Illinois, 1971.

Entwistle, N., and Entwistle, A. "Contrasting Forms of Understanding for Degree Examinations." Higher Education, 1991, 22, 205–227.

Fishkin, J. *Democracy and Deliberation: New Directions for Democratic Reform.* New Haven, Conn.: Yale University Press, 1991.

Fishkin, J. *The Voice of the People: Public Opinion and Democracy.* New Haven, Conn.: Yale University Press, 1995.

Gastil, J. "Democratic Education and the National Issues Forum." Unpublished doctoral dissertation, Department of Communication Arts, University of Wisconsin, 1994.

Gastil, J. "A Thought-Piece on Deliberation." Report prepared for the Kettering Foundation by the Institute for Public Policy. Albuquerque: University of New Mexico, 1995.

Gastil, J., Adams, G., and Jenkins-Smith, H. "Understanding Public Deliberation." Report prepared for the Charles F. Kettering Foundation by the Institute for Public Policy. Albuquerque: University of New Mexico, 1995.

Halpern, D. F. *Thought and Knowledge: An Introduction to Critical Thinking.* (3rd ed.) Mahwah, N.J.: Erlbaum, 1996.

Holt, M. E., Milton, J., and McCall, M. "Creating New Public Spaces: Moderating a National Issues Forum on the Web." Paper presented at the International Association of Facilitators Conference, San Clara, Calif., Jan. 14–19, 1998.

Holt, M. E., Rees, F., Swenson, J. D., and Kleiber, P. B. "Evolution of Evaluation for Critical, Reflective, and Deliberative Discourse: National Issues Forums Online." Paper presented at the Special Interest Group on Assessment and Evaluation of the European Association for Research on Learning and Instruction, Athens, Greece, Aug. 26–30, 1997.

Hustedde, R. J. "An Evaluation of the National Issues Forum Methodology for Stimulating Deliberation in Rural Kentucky." *Journal of the Community Development Society,* 1996, 27(2), 197–210.

King, P. M., and Kitchener, K. S. *Developing Reflective Judgment: Understanding and Promoting Intellectual Growth and Critical Thinking in Adolescents and Adults.* San Francisco: Jossey-Bass, 1994.

Kleiber, P. B, Holt, M., and Swenson, J. D. "The Electronic Forum Handbook: Study Circles in Cyberspace." [http://www.journalism.wisc.edu/cpn/sections/tools/manuals/electronic-handbookI.html]. Pomfret, Conn.: Study Circles Resource Center, 1995.

Kohlberg, L. *The Psychology of Moral Development: The Nature and Validation of Moral Stages.* San Francisco: HarperCollins, 1984.

Mathews, D. *Politics for People: Finding a Responsible Public Voice.* Urbana: University of Illinois Press, 1994.

McCall, M., and Szerdy, J. (1998). "Facilitate.com: Virtual Conferencing Teamware." [http://www.facilitate.com/]. Feb. 1998.

McKenzie, R. H. "Experiential Education and Civic Learning." *National Society for Experiential Education Quarterly,* 1996, 22(2), 1, 20–23.

Mishoe, S. C. "Critical Thinking in Respiratory Care Practice." Unpublished doctoral dissertation, Department of Adult Education, University of Georgia, Athens, 1994.

Paul, R. W. *Critical Thinking: What Every Person Needs to Survive in a Rapidly Changing World.* Rohnert Park, Calif.: Center for Critical Thinking and Moral Critique, Sonoma State University, 1990.

Perry, W. G. *Forms of Intellectual and Ethical Development in the College Years: A Scheme.* Austin, Tex.: Holt, Rinehart and Winston, 1970.

Piaget, J. *The Child and Reality* (A. Rosin, trans.). New York: Viking, 1974.

Pratkanis, A. R., and Turner, M. E. "Persuasion and Democracy: Strategies for Increasing Deliberative Participation and Enacting Social Change." *Journal of Social Issues,* 1996, 52(1), 197–205.

Roschelle, J. "What Should Collaborative Technology Be? A Perspective from Dewey and Situated Learning." [http://www.cica.indiana.edu/csc195/outlook39_roschelle.html]. 1992.

Shaffer, C. R., and Anundsen, K. *Creating Community Anywhere: Finding Support and Connection in a Fragmented World.* New York: Putnam, 1993.

Watson, G., and Glaser, E. M. *Watson-Glaser Critical Thinking Appraisal Manual.* Orlando: Harcourt Brace, 1964.

Yankelovich, D. *Coming to Public Judgment: Making Democracy Work in a Complex World.* Syracuse, N.Y.: Syracuse University Press, 1991.

MARGARET E. HOLT *is an associate professor of adult education at the University of Georgia, Athens, and an associate with the Charles F. Kettering Foundation.*

PAMELA B. KLEIBER *serves as department head of University System of Georgia Independent Study at the University of Georgia Center for Continuing Education, Athens.*

JILL DIANNE SWENSON *is an associate professor of journalism in the Television-Radio Department at Ithaca College, Ithaca, New York.*

E. FRANCES REES *is a graduate of the doctoral program in the Department of Adult Education at the University of Georgia, Athens.*

JUDY MILTON *is a doctoral student in the Department of Adult Education at the University of Georgia, Athens.*

On-line courses require new strategies for design and delivery. This chapter examines pedagogical, organizational, and institutional issues that must be resolved for effective Internet-based instruction.

On-Line Education:
A Study of Emerging Pedagogy

Lynne Schrum

Students are beginning to expect access to new models for lifelong learning. Many institutions are feeling pressure to offer on-line courses, yet most faculty and administrators are ill prepared to do so effectively. This chapter identifies significant issues in the development of such courses, including ways to create interaction between and among learners, drawing on research, on the experiences of the author in teaching on-line courses, and on interviews with instructors, potential instructors, and students of on-line courses.

Examples of traditional courses offered with a variety of telecommunications methods (e-mail, computer conferencing, satellite delivery) have been discussed in the literature (Harasim, 1993; Hiltz, 1990; Rice-Lively, 1994; Schrum, 1992; Sproull and Kiesler, 1991). In the majority of these courses, instruction is delivered entirely or principally via computer-mediated communications (CMC). These and other studies suggest that this form of education is effective for well-motivated students. More important, they indicate that traditional courses cannot be delivered effectively through CMC without significant changes.

The impact of on-line courses has only begun to be investigated. To date, the traditional distance education literature has focused on the design and implementation of correspondence, compressed video, or satellite broadcast delivery courses. That literature provides some parallels, but does not directly inform the design and development of on-line courses.

Large numbers of community colleges, continuing education centers, universities, and private training enterprises have expanded their programs to include courses delivered partially or entirely on-line, and many other organizations are considering implementing such courses. Institutions are feeling

NEW DIRECTIONS FOR ADULT AND CONTINUING EDUCATION, no. 78, Summer 1998 © Jossey-Bass Publishers

particularly vulnerable because the advantage of location no longer ensures them a market based on geography.

Additionally, the technologies designed and promoted by the computer and media industries are constantly changing, with marketing appearing to drive demand at least as strongly as customer requirements. Institutions are often unsure what innovations are necessary. Educators must avoid being distracted by superficial changes while at the same time using appropriate technologies to create courses that are pedagogically sound, organizationally strong, and institutionally supported.

Lessons from the Literature

The literature reports an increasing number of courses and degrees delivered entirely through CMC, including many traditional undergraduate classes. In some circumstances the technology is only a repository, merely holding the materials (Boston, 1992), but in others there is evidence that the technology itself becomes the environment for new forms of learning (Dede, 1995).

Distance learning in various forms has been around for a long time, but until recently it was not feasible to offer on-line courses to large numbers of individuals. Currently military, business, and nontraditional educational providers have begun to investigate the potential of the Web for on-line education. Growing numbers of nontraditional students must overcome concerns about time, distance, and money that traditional students do not have. On-line learning offers potential solutions to these issues.

Traditional distance learning was based on passive media (paper, audio, and video broadcast) and was frequently conducted with each learner corresponding only with an instructor. Internet technologies offer the opportunity to improve on this model through increased communication, interactivity, and collaboration. Harasim (1990) summarized the characteristics of on-line courses as place and time independence, many-to-many communication, collaborative learning, and dependence on text-based communications to promote thoughtful and reflective commentary. Other advantages of this type of distance learning are synchronous and asynchronous communication, access to and from geographically isolated communities, and sharing of cultural diversity.

Development of an on-line educational environment is not a trivial task. Wiesenberg and Hutton (1996) identified three major challenges for the designer: increased time for delivery of the course (they estimate two or three times what is necessary for a traditional course), creating a on-line community, and encouraging students to become independent learners. They also reported less interaction than expected from participants in an on-line course.

Reid and Woolf (1996) discuss the benefits of integrating on-line components into traditional classes, such as accessibility, learner control, heightened communication, access to worldwide resources, and the potential for a more student-centered environment. Heeren and Lewis (1997) suggest matching the media with the task, keeping lean media (for example, e-mail) for tasks that do not require much interaction, and reserving rich media for things that require more interaction and broader spectrum of activity (face-to-face).

Communication through technology has the potential to change the way in which people behave, according to Lea and Spears (1991). They identified a change in informal and formal talk and individuals' loss of identity and deindividuation. Tatar, Foster, and Bobrow (1991) suggest that group work is not just individuals working at computers at the same time, but means "giving participants the ability to judge when it is appropriate to overlap, just as they judge the efficacy" of adding to verbal conversations (p. 77). Group members need support to learn and act out their roles in these situations (Olson and Bly, 1991).

On-line learners report attitudes of greater control and responsibility toward their learning; students also find that writing demands greater reflection than speaking (Harasim, 1990; Rohfeld and Hiemstra, 1994). Several studies have looked at on-line components of traditional courses and concluded that they substantially increase the communication between the teacher and the students and among the students, when compared to similar writing classes without computer communication (Hartman and others, 1991; Hiltz, 1990; Schrum, 1995; Schrum and Lamb, 1996).

Electronic communication thus appears to foster collaboration and group interactions. In a study of distributed research, in which individuals who were geographically distant from each other collaborated on a research project, Olson and Bly (1991) concluded that "interpersonal computing supports people communicating and working together through the computer; it includes tools to support interaction separated by time and/or space as well as face-to-face interaction and meetings. . . . Work forced the boundaries of social place to extend beyond the boundaries of physical place" (p. 81).

Groupware is software that supports and augments group work. However, most investigations have focused on those capabilities useful in business settings, particularly among colocated populations who used the software synchronously, often in group decision activities (Valacich, Dennis, and Nunamaker, 1991). The literature is now beginning to expand the concept of groupware to include asynchronous and geographically distributed activities.

Strategies for Designing On-line Instruction

Data gathered from personal experience and interviews suggest that specific student characteristics are associated with success in on-line courses. Students identified themselves as successful when they had strong reasons for signing up for a course, moved through the lessons fairly rapidly, had support from their family, were independent learners, and began with a certain level of technological knowledge and experience. They also reported that their continued use of information technology depends on its ease and cost of access, the time available for practice and experimentation, and support for risk taking.

On-line courses appear to best meet the needs of students who are unable to attend a university or whose university does not offer the desired course, those in remote locations or in gridlocked urban areas, those already comfortable with computers, and those who prefer to work individually or without time and location constraints. These student characteristics should be considered when designing an on-line educational experience.

These findings can be used to shape decision making about the creation of courses. Guidelines can be divided into the areas of pedagogical, organizational, and institutional issues.

Pedagogical Concerns. Pedagogical issues include the identification of learning goals, philosophical changes in teaching and learning, reconceptualization of the teacher's role, evaluation of student and instructor, and the stimulation of interactivity.

Before decisions can be made about delivery or models, instructors must make pedagogical decisions about the goals of a course. The salient questions when creating an educational experience have always been, What is the purpose of this course? and What are the instructional and personal goals of this course? In general, educators are adept at answering such questions.

Duchastel (1996–97) suggests a continuum that helps an instructor extend the traditional classroom model to one better fitted to electronic processes and global resources. He argues for moving from "static content to specifying goals to pursue; one answer to accepting a diversity of outcomes; re-presenting knowledge to requesting production of knowledge; evaluating at the product level to looking to the task level; individual efforts to building learning teams; one classroom to encouraging global communities" (p. 224).

The course designer may choose to redesign an existing course or create a new course, but it is unwise to simply transfer an old course to this new medium. The structure of the course, the planning for educational and personal needs, and the teacher's role must all be reconceived. The designer will have to determine what actions will promote the active and independent learning characteristic of successful on-line courses. Relevant materials and negotiated assignments help to ensure participation, involvement, and action.

One way to begin might include taking an assignment that has proved useful and authentic in traditional classroom use. This might be creating a small project, identifying specific content, or synthesizing activities. Now the instructor must consider how this could work as an on-line experience. Would necessary materials be available to each student? Would the activity require students to work independently, to gather resources, and then to present them on-line to the rest of the class? Should students take turns having the responsibility for organizing and leading a discussion? Perhaps the most significant challenge is one of instructors' giving themselves permission to experiment, fail, and try again. Feedback from learners is crucial in this iterative process.

On-line teaching requires the instructor to rethink the evaluation process as well. Evaluation must be ongoing and continual; relying on one midterm and a final paper would put students at a disadvantage. The instructor should become familiar with each student's work through a series of activities. Without visual cues, the instructor may be unaware of a student's confusion or misunderstanding. It may be wise to plan several points during the term when students will provide anonymous feedback about the course. Some faculty include one question each week that requires students to discuss aspects of the content, interactions, and affective qualities of their on-line experience.

Creating Interactivity in an On-line Environment. In traditional courses, the amount of interactivity varies widely. Potentially, learners can interact in three ways: with the content, the instructor, and the other learners. Yet many traditional courses center on lecture and note taking. The on-line environment offers possibilities for broadening interaction, and its differences from classroom teaching have compelled many instructors to explore these possibilities.

Students can interact with content in a variety of ways. However, as in most areas of learning, self-regulation and active participation are essential. The instructor might require students to post comments on readings, or provide links to previously evaluated Internet resources. Access to the instructor's personal notes and pertinent questions can help focus the readings. Students can also post other products of their work, such as essays, scanned images, and Web pages.

The instructor and each student are likely to develop their own style of interaction. Laurillard (1993) describes four ways of supporting interaction with learners in an electronic environment. These include a reliance on discursive language to understand each other's conceptions; adaptiveness, so that the focus can shift as the students' needs shift; frequent activities that allow students to demonstrate their understandings; and recurrent reflection on the students' work.

Collaborative student work requires another level of consideration. Groups might solve a problem, create a simulation for others, design a product, or complete a task. These activities may or may not be mandatory, and the groups may be self-selecting or may be created heterogeneously to simulate a work situation. Some instructors have students post the type of project they would like to do and also list some of their work styles to facilitate group formation. (For example, individuals who are comfortable finishing at the very last minute may not work well with those who wish to be finished a week ahead of time.)

Finally, the instructor must decide whether student interactions will occur synchronously or asynchronously. For most tasks that require thought and reflection, the synchronous model may not be very useful. Individuals using chat software report frustration in keeping track of what others are typing and being able to type their own contributions. Frequently, one person who can type very rapidly dominates the conversation. Also, simultaneous meetings may not be viable for all participants. Synchronous activities require careful structures, advance organizers, and monitoring.

Organizational Issues. Organizational issues revolve around timing, inclusion of face-to-face components (if possible), group interactions, and prerequisites.

First, a decision must be made about how much of the course will be online. Is this to be a Web-enhanced course or a Web-only course? The on-line component can range from occasional electronic assignments that supplement traditional class meetings to an on-line course with two or three face-to-face meetings to a course held entirely on-line. Obviously many factors may be outside the instructor's control; for example, if the course is intended for a distant audience, meeting face to face may not be an option.

Another question concerns the timing of the course. Will it begin and end on a schedule—perhaps coinciding with the school or university calendar? Or will it be conducted as a completely independent study? Many students benefit from the routine and structure that accompany a traditional course schedule, while others are frustrated by the need to move either more quickly or more slowly than they would prefer. Whatever the decision, it is important to inform the participants of their responsibilities for the course.

As on-line courses proliferate, students will increasingly be able to choose their own option for the timing of the course. Boise State University offers an entire Masters program on-line, and the participants typically do not meet each other until graduation day. Eastern Montana College offers a course with no face-to-face meetings but with a structured time line. Many universities, including the University of Georgia, have explored a model that has students meet at the beginning and end of the course, follow a university schedule, receive assignments weekly, and hold discussions on-line. Rochester Institute of Technology offers several of its undergraduate courses on-line and follows the traditional calendar.

Another organizational determination must be made about the types of assignments and interactions that are to be included. These may range from group projects created and delivered on-line to completely individual assignments. If everyone is moving through the course at the same time, could the interaction be enhanced by one or more synchronous activities, when all students are on-line at the same time? As research on one graduate course demonstrated, even in the case of independent on-line lessons, it is useful to require students to interact with their colleagues in some way (Schrum, 1992). The use of groupware as an instructional tool has potential to enhance the nature and perceptions of interaction in on-line courses (Schrum and Lamb, 1996).

Other organizational issues must be considered. Group size may influence communications patterns, but it also significantly affects the workload of the teacher. Teaching on-line courses requires a great deal of time—to answer mail, to manage data, and to respond to postings. It has been suggested that fifteen to twenty students is a manageable group for interaction and also for instructors; however, some institutions believe that on-line courses should handle large numbers of students at one time. Are extra tutors available to assist, or is it possible to team-teach a course? One instructor has decided that the team approach allows the widest possible flexibility and offers the best support for the students.

Instructors should specify the prerequisite skills expected of the students. Individuals with little computer experience are likely to be less successful in on-line courses because they can spend enormous amounts of time completing the most basic of word processing tasks.

Finally, although some educators prefer to determine their curriculum and activities as a course evolves, in an on-line course it is especially important that students be given a list of assignments, readings, and expectations at the beginning. Introductory activities must be appropriate for computer novices and experts alike, and rules for netiquette should be established early on.

Institutional Issues. To succeed as providers of on-line courses, institutions must address issues of faculty incentives, access and equity, credit decisions, ongoing evaluation, and technical support for students and teachers.

Many institutions see on-line instruction as a means to raise revenues in an increasingly competitive marketplace (Phelps, Wells, Ashworth, and Hahn, 1991). But long-term success will depend largely on recognition in the promotion and tenure process for faculty who create and teach on-line courses. Institutional support for innovative practices requires that time be allowed for design and development. While acceptance of on-line courses is growing, many institutions still do not count their preparation as part of an instructor's load.

Other institutional issues concern the amount and types of credit offered for on-line courses, and students' ability to use such credit for graduate or undergraduate degrees, salary increments, or other types of certification. Will students taking an on-line course be supported in registration, transcript processing, and other administrative services in the same ways as traditional students? Who will bear the expense of network connectivity associated with on-line courses? Will modems or computers be loaned to students who cannot afford them? How will students at a geographic distance gain access to materials on campus?

It is essential that an evaluative component be included for every course. Is the course pedagogically sound? Has it accomplished its goals? Is the organizational structure appropriate and equitable? Did the institution offer the support necessary for students and for the educator? Did unique problems arise from the on-line nature of the course?

Another issue is evaluation of the instructor. Currently most instructors are evaluated by their students. However, in an on-line environment it may be more difficult for students to assess some aspects of their teachers' performance. This calls for a more substantial and perhaps collaborative evaluation of the instructor by all stakeholders.

Conclusion

This chapter provides an overview of the issues surrounding the emerging pedagogy of on-line education. Teachers, students, and administrators are all struggling to balance goals, needs, and resources, but clearly the desire and opportunities exist to create new forms of educational experience. The following recommendations may be useful to individuals and organizations undertaking that process.

1. Create a team of developers that includes a technical person, a subject matter expert, an instructional designer, and a student.
2. Allow time for this team to explore, experiment, and evaluate their activity.
3. Create a mini-course that learners can take to test hardware, learn software skills, experience on-line education, and determine if it is an effective learning environment for them.
4. Begin with a few courses and expand gradually. Continuously revise and improve courses, using failures as opportunities to learn. Reward early adopters for their willingness to take risks.

Educators must consider pedagogical, policy, and support issues before plunging into on-line courses. Further, as a community of scholars and educators, we should strive to create more avenues for sharing our experiences and research, be willing to describe difficulties, and accept feedback from learners. Recently a colleague mentioned that, while there is nothing wrong with reinventing the wheel, perhaps we do not all have to reinvent square wheels. If ever an aspect of education required collaboration, this one certainly does.

References

Boston, R. L. "Remote Delivery of Instruction via the PC and Modem: What Have We Learned?" *American Journal of Distance Education,* 1992, 6(3), 45–57.

Dede, C. "The Transformation of Distance Education to Distributed Learning." InTRO. [http://129.7.160.78/InTRO.html]. July 1995.

Duchastel, P. "A Web-Based Model for University Instruction." *Journal of Educational Technology Systems,* 1996–97, 25(3), 221–228.

Harasim, L. M. "Online Education: An Environment for Collaboration and Intellectual Amplification." In L. M. Harasim (ed.), *Online Education: Perspectives on a New Environment.* New York: Praeger, 1990.

Harasim, L. M. (ed.). *Global Networks: Computers and International Communication.* Cambridge, Mass.: MIT Press, 1993.

Hartman, K., Neuwirth, C. M., Kiesler, S., Sproull, L., Cochran, C., Palmquist, M., and Zubrow, D. "Patterns of Social Interaction and Learning to Write: Some Effects of Network Technologies." *Written Communication,* 1991, 8(1), 79–113.

Heeren, E., and Lewis, R. "Selecting Communication Media for Distributed Communities." *Journal of Computer Assisted Learning,* 1997, 13(2), 85–98.

Hiltz, R. S. "Evaluating the Virtual Classroom." In L. M. Harasim (ed.), *Online Education: Perspectives on a New Environment.* New York: Praeger, 1990.

Laurillard, D. *Rethinking University Teaching: A Framework for the Effective Use of Educational Technology.* New York: Routledge, 1993.

Lea, M., and Spears, R. "Computer Mediated Communication, De-Individuation and Group Decision-Making." In S. Greenberg (ed.), *Computer Supported Cooperative Work and Groupware.* Orlando: Academic Press, 1991.

Olson, M. H., and Bly, S. A. "The Portland Experience: A Report on a Distributed Research Group." In S. Greenberg (ed.), *Computer Supported Cooperative Work and Groupware.* Orlando: Academic Press, 1991.

Phelps, R. H., Wells, R. A., Ashworth, R. L., and Hahn, H. A. "Effectiveness and Costs of Distance Education Using Computer-Mediated Communication." *American Journal of Distance Education,* 1991, 5(3), 7–19.

Reid, J. E. and Woolf, P. "Online Curriculum Development at Shorter College: A Report from the Field." [http://www.caso.com/iu/articles/reid02.html]. 1996.

Rice-Lively, M. L. "Wired Warp and Woof: An Ethnographic Study of a Networking Class." *Internet Research,* 1994, 4(4), 20–35.

Rohfeld, R. W., and Hiemstra, R. "Moderating Discussions in the Electronic Classroom." In Z. L. Berge and M. P. Collins (eds.), *Computer-Mediated Communication and the Online Classroom, Vol. III: Distance Learning.* Cresskill, N.J.: Hampton Press, 1994.

Schrum, L. "Professional Development in the Information Age: An Online Experience." *Educational Technology,* 1992, 32(12), 49–53.

Schrum, L. "Educators and the Internet: A Case Study of Professional Development." *Computers and Education,* 1995, 24(3), 221–228.

Schrum, L., and Lamb, T. A. "Groupware for Collaborative Learning: A Research Perspective on Processes, Opportunities, and Obstacles." *Journal of Universal Computer Science,* 1996, 2(10), 717–731 [http://www.iicm.edu/jucs].

Sproull, L., and Kiesler, S. *Connections: New Ways of Working in the Networked Organization.* Cambridge, Mass.: MIT Press, 1991.

Tatar, D. G., Foster, G., and Bobrow, D. G. "Design for Conversation: Lessons from Cognoter." In S. Greenberg (ed.), *Computer Supported Cooperative Work and Groupware.* Orlando: Academic Press, 1991.

Valacich, J. S., Dennis, A. R., and Nunamaker, J. F. "Electronic Meeting Support: The GroupSystems Concept." In S. Greenberg (ed.), *Computer Supported Cooperative Work and Groupware.* Orlando: Academic Press, 1991.

Wiesenberg, F., and Hutton, S. "Teaching a Graduate Program using Computer-Mediated Conferencing Software." *Journal of Distance Education,* 1996, 11(1), 83–100.

LYNNE SCHRUM is associate professor of instructional technology at the University of Georgia, Athens.

Power, access, control, privacy, and equity are among the many ethical concerns that face those who teach or learn on the Internet. Despite proclamations of educational progress through technology, the potentials for harm cannot be ignored or underestimated.

Ethical Considerations in Internet-Based Adult Education

Margaret E. Holt

Adult educators, like everyone else in the teaching and learning enterprise, are well advised to weigh ethical issues attached to Internet technologies. Some problems may be unique to these systems and tools, yet most are simply familiar dilemmas exacerbated by qualities such as speed, access, ease of manipulation, and scope of dissemination. Concerns for privacy, access, and intellectual property rights, for example, are hardly unique to the Internet, but risks may be magnified by the power and reach of electronic systems. As Resnick comments, "The sad fact is that the problems of the real world have penetrated the Internet" (quoted in Weber, 1997, p. R29). The technology genie is out of the bottle, and there's no stuffing it back inside.

Until recently, monitors in the halls of higher education appeared to detect little change in the way learning was to be delivered to students. Ample chalk, theater seating, and a lecture in hand seemed sufficient. Environmental scanners did not initially detect the technological transformation that was coming, while others expressed skepticism (not without some justification) that educational institutions could move swiftly enough to keep pace. In 1993, Landow observed, "It took only twenty-five years for the overhead projector to make it from the bowling alley to the classroom. I'm optimistic about academic computing; I've begun to see computers in bowling alleys" (p. 161).

But the technological changes brought about by the Internet will not slouch along over a quarter of a century. Whirlwind infiltration of hardware and software tools is already creating a turbulent environment in all of education. Technophiles and Luddites speak such different dialects that at best there is a failure to communicate and at worst dysfunction and hostility. These divisions are occurring within individuals as well as between them. Already

NEW DIRECTIONS FOR ADULT AND CONTINUING EDUCATION, no. 78, Summer 1998 © Jossey-Bass Publishers

specialties in psychiatry are emerging to diagnose and treat technology addicts. Describing his own "Internet addiction," Ditlea (1995) contends, "Nothing can help the recovering modemaholic like F2F (face-to-face) meetings, where experiences like mine can be related. . . . Such meetings don't exist yet but I'm convinced the time is near when a 12-step virtual community will help countless others like me living one day at a time—off-line" (p. 12).

Certain ethical problems associated with Internet technology concern psychological well-being, while other risks are societal. E-mail, for example, while touted for its ease in disseminating ideas, allows both good and bad information to be transmitted with equal speed. The same technology that might help us to be more democratic, equitable, inclusive, and safe can just as easily facilitate incivility, offensive and violent speech, and widely disseminated declarations of hate toward individuals or groups (Raney, 1998). Orlikowski and Hoffman (1997) note that the deployment of e-mail typically produces unintended, emergent consequences in organizations: "An example of an anticipated change is the implementation of e-mail software that accomplishes its intended aim to facilitate increased, quicker communication among organizational members. An example of an emergent change is the use of the e-mail network as an informal grapevine disseminating rumors throughout an organization. The use of e-mail is typically not planned or anticipated when the network is implemented but often emerges tacitly over time in particular organizational contexts" (pp. 12–13).

Today, educational organizations are being transformed by the intended and unintended effects of technology. Even as its ubiquity begins to render it invisible, Internet technology demands continuous ethical and moral reflection (Reed and Sork, 1990). In a series of influential critiques, Postman (1985, 1992) has warned that we may be "amused to death" or mentally numbed if we fail to recognize and reflect upon the capacity of a "technopoly." Olcott (1997) observes "Mass deployment of technology in all spheres of human endeavor affects the lives of many. The crucial questions, however, cannot be answered if they are not being asked. We educators (particularly those who control technology) have a responsibility to reflect upon the ethical and moral issues around technology. We are a voice for successive generations, for teaching and learning, and for promoting public discourse about the relative merits of technology in education and society. Mr. Orwell would certainly agree with this assertion and would echo, that 'just because we can, doesn't mean we should' is a good place to begin anew."

Olcott also warns us to be aware of a false sense of progress with technology. He contends, "the two words, progress and technology, are not always synonyms. . . . We must pause long enough to step out of the technological maze and define the social boundaries of technology in education, society, and our lives rather than creating a culture permeated by what I call 'techapathy.'"

Clearly, scholarship and research are transformed by the ability to search and access tremendous quantities of on-line text and data. However, students may not be skilled in checking the accuracy or authenticity of the information they discover. Misinformation on the Internet includes incomplete information, pranks, contradictions, out-of-date information, improperly translated data, unauthorized revisions, factual errors, biased information, and scholarly misconduct (Fitzgerald, 1996). Cut-and-paste editing makes it easier for those less ethically inclined to take information out of context and manipulate other people's work. Links to or attributions of original sources are frequently deleted or omitted by Internet plagiarists. Creative individuals enjoy the access, freedom, and flexibility to easily alter many forms of audiovisual material.

Anonymity, privacy, and confidentiality are at the forefront of ethical and legal deliberations about the Internet. Only a few scholars have attempted to examine the new meanings of human subjects requirements for research when those subjects are participants in electronic forums and conversations (Schrum and Harris, 1996). As yet, standards or norms for transmitting data electronically, securing privacy, or publishing works in repositories are scarce. Is electronic speech public or private? How is it protected? Who owns the data? An adult education student in a 1996 seminar at the University of Georgia expressed these convictions about ownership on-line (cited here with her permission):

> The written word is owned by the writer and with that ownership comes responsibility. Writers are responsible for the putting forth defensible ideas, for instance. On the other hand, the readers of the written word bring expectations. We expect that the words we read represent commitment on the part of the writer. We never naturally assume tentativeness on a writer's part even though this may be a reality. We expect the written words to fall together cohesively and coherently and to reflect the best thinking of the writer at the time. We even expect the words to endure over time. After all, since the words on the page have permanence we bring tacit expectations that the ideas beneath the words have permanence as well. The responsibilities and expectations that accompany writing place pressure on the writer. It is this pressure that discourages me from participating in a virtual community. If I am not ready to assume the responsibility because my ideas are not, in fact, well-developed enough for public sharing, then I am reluctant to send my words into Cyberspace for all to read and judge.

A related example of the ambivalence of students toward Internet-based instruction was offered by a professor on the ALNTALK on-line conference hosted by Vanderbilt University:

> I had an interesting situation while teaching with FirstClass conferencing in a graduate education course last year. I logged on at 11:30 one night and checked to see who else was online. One of my students was so I invited her for a 'chat.' She told me she was having problems with some homework so I helped her online for about 30 minutes. I was very pleased with this experience but then later found out that she was worried that I could monitor her at any time that I wanted. She thought I could actually read what she was writing while she wrote

it in her own home on her home computer. I really took this as a message to inform my students more about what I could not do as the instructor using the technology [Bullock, 1997].

These comments illustrate not only the ethical consideration of owner-ship of ideas, but also that of individual freedom to choose to participate in Internet-based educational activities. The instructor who believes that she has a responsibility to assure her students are competent in the use of information technology faces a dilemma. Is it fair to require students to use technological tools when no clear consensus of opinion exists on the effectiveness or value of the learning resulting from such use? As Gilbert (1996) observes, "Unfor-tunately, there is no clear, irrefutable quantitative evidence of the superiority of education uses of information technology; and if information technology were certain to provide a simple solution to the 'education problem' it would already have been reported in every news medium." He adds that it is too soon for generalizations about the effectiveness of this mode of learning, nor is much known about the relationship between these types of learning modes and learning styles and motivations.

Another longtime ethical problem in academe that has been given new intensity by the Internet is academic honesty. Does the ready availability of searchable information increase the probability that students will steal the intel-lectual work of others and present it as their own? Innumerable Internet sites offer research papers for sale. Those tempted to plagiarize need only elemen-tary surfing skills to find sites named "School sucks," "Cheater.com," "Term Paper Warehouse," "Essays for Sale," and "Recycled Papers," to name but a few sources of other people's ideas on thousands of topics. Papers are available in multiple languages, and students can even request papers that are said to be consistent with their recorded performance levels. For example, a student can request an "A" paper or a "C" paper, to prevent instructors from suspecting pla-giarism if the paper is found inconsistent with past performance.

In addition to sensitizing students to matters of accuracy and honesty when using the Internet, instructors must pay thoughtful attention to the new power relationships it defines. Winner (1995) comments, "To invent a new technology requires that (in some way or another) society also invents the kinds of people who will use it; older practices, relationships and ways of defining people's identities fall by the wayside; new practices, relationships and identities take root."

Despite concerns about mandatory participation in on-line conferencing, researchers at the University of Georgia and Ithaca College found that reflec-tive thinking was advanced for most participants in on-line National Issues Forums (see Chapter Five in this volume). Evaluations of these forums reflect a great range in learner satisfaction with the experience. A number of the par-ticipants found the verbal requirements of the forums constructive in helping stretch their abilities to express ideas in writing, while others found the exclu-sive emphasis on writing limiting, as other indicators of viewpoints such as body language and facial expressions were absent. With limited research available to assess the nature of reflective thinking, deliberation, and discourse in Internet-based adult education, what is a responsible and fair position for instructors to assume regarding mandatory use of such technology in learning activities? How can instructors assess and grade student performance in group learning activities on the Internet? Should they be graded?

If students are not required to use Internet resources, will they be passed over for better jobs when they graduate? Gilbert (1996) wrote that students will be jeopardized and in some cases noncompetitive for careers if they do not integrate technology into their learning. Without a doubt, there are increasing numbers of jobs for which people lacking technological skills need not apply.

Already, intentionally or not, technology adopters have demonstrated a power to include and exclude, to assimilate and to isolate. In a world where an uneven distribution of education resources continues to prevail, it is hardly surprising that access to the Internet is also unevenly distributed. Demographic studies indicate that, compared to the general population, a disproportionately large number of active Internet users have college degrees, suggesting that access tends to break down along the lines of prior educational and economic success (Hoffman, Kalsbeek, and Novak, 1996). In a talk to a Teaching, Learning, and Technology Roundtable workshop, Reed Hundt, then chair of the Federal Communications Commission, labeled this dichotomous potential a "cutting wedge"—rather than the "cutting edge"—within society (Gilbert, 1996).

The haves-and-have-nots debate about Internet-based education is highly polarized. Some view the technology as a new means to include people who have traditionally been marginalized and oppressed, while others see such inclusion as a moot point as long as economic and structural factors go unaddressed. It seems clear that distance education technology can be used to facilitate hegemony if those in authority wish to maintain a segregation of learners by offering marginalized groups access to learning only via distance systems. Shaffer and Anundsen (1993) comment that to those who cannot access and use computers, those who can appear to be an elite, private group. Gilbert (1996) argues, "It is much too early to claim that offering only distance education options to any segment of society determined by rural location or lack of wealth can truly provide something like quality of educational opportunity."

The 1997 American Internet User Survey reports that "most users pay for their own access" (Miller and Clemente, 1997), raising the question of the extent to which economic barriers prevent people from becoming Internet users. According to Fortner (1995), excluding those who cannot afford information tools is one way to "excommunicate" individuals. He adds excess and choice as two other contributors to disconnection. Excess, or an overload of information that seems impossible to manage and muddle through, will deter some potential participants. Others, committed to voluntary simplicity, will make a considered decision not to invest themselves because they have determined that life in front of a computer is not something they need or want.

While not necessarily nostalgic, their "no thanks" attitude toward the Internet is similar to the way some people have opted not to complicate their lives with VCRs, microwave ovens, and cellular phones.

Statistics presented by Bolles in the 1997 *Job-Hunting on the Internet Guide* indicate that over 60 percent of American households do not have a home computer, more than 75 percent do not have a modem, more than 80 percent are not actually on-line, and almost 100 percent (99.93 percent) do not hunt for jobs on-line. The report goes on to state that 75 percent of Americans do not have access to the Internet at work or school, almost 80 percent never access the Internet, and only 8 percent "actually access the Internet regularly" (p. 4). While other sources present different numbers, and while Internet usage is a fast-moving and difficult-to-measure target, it is clear that for now only a limited portion of the population makes effective use of the Internet. Revisiting the issues posed by Fortner, the significant question is whether such limited access is a matter of choice or lack of possibility due to location or expense. Some students have greater access because they are wealthier, while others have greater access because they attend institutions that have committed more resources to these tools. Age is also a factor, according to Gilbert (1996): "The number of part-time and older students who have jobs is growing rapidly; but they are less likely to have these new technologies comfortably available for educational use at home or in their workplaces. They also have less time to use public access facilities on a campus."

Adult educators must be alert and attentive to the unavoidable ethical and legal issues surrounding Internet-based instruction. The exponential rate at which new hardware and software are introduced is likely to frustrate any attempts to standardize educational practices. Nonetheless, it is critical that the adult and continuing education field continue to be identified as a discipline that respects the dignity of persons by promoting and observing standards of ethical behavior.

References

Bolles, R. N. *Job-Hunting on the Internet.* Berkeley, Calif.: Ten Speed Press, 1997.

Bullock, C. D. "Students' Perceptions of Privacy with Conferencing." [http://www.aln.org /forums/Thread.cfm?CFApp=2&&Message_ID=4280&_#Message4280]. ALNTALK, Sept. 24, 1997.

Ditlea, S. "Report from the Front: How to Beat Internet Addiction." *Interactive Age,* Feb. 13, 1995, p. 12.

Fitzgerald, M. A. "Misinformation on the Internet: Applying Evaluation Skills to Online Information." Unpublished manuscript. Athens: University of Georgia, 1996.

Fortner, R. S. "Excommunication in the Information Society." *Critical Studies in Mass Communication,* 1995, *12*, 133–154.

Gilbert, S. W. "Re-Focus on Learning and Teaching: The Educational Uses of Information Technology for Everyone." [http://www.sunsite.unc.edu/horizon/gems/listarchive/96list /0216.html]. Horizon List, July 4, 1996.

Hoffman, D. L., Kalsbeek, W. D., and Novak, T. P. "Internet and Web Use in the United States: Baselines for Commercial Development." [http://www2000.ogsm.vanderbilt.edu /baseline/internet.demos.july9.1996.html]. Nashville, Tenn.: Project 2000, Owen Graduate School of Management, Vanderbilt University, July 1996.

Landow, G. *Hypertext: The Convergence of Contemporary Critical Theory and Technology.* Baltimore: Johns Hopkins University Press, 1993.

Miller, T. E., and Clemente, P. C. "1997 American Internet User Survey." [http://etrg.findsvp.com/internet/findf.html]. New York: FIND/SVP, 1997.

Olcott, D., Jr. "Where Are You George Orwell? We Got the Year . . . Missed the Message." Online document; e-mail the command GET DEOSNEWS 97–00004 to LISTSERV@ PSUVM.PSU.EDU. DEOSNEWS, 1997, 7(4).

Orlikowski, W. J., and Hoffman, J. D. "An Improvisational Model for Change Management: The Case of Groupware Technologies." *Sloan Management Review,* 1997, *38*(2), 11–21.

Postman, N. *Amusing Ourselves to Death: Public Discourse in the Age of Show Business.* New York: Viking, 1985.

Postman, N. *Technopoly: The Surrender of Culture to Technology.* New York: Knopf, 1992.

Raney, R. F. "E-mail Trial May Set U.S. Precedent." [http://www.nytimes.com/library/cyber/week/012198hate.html]. *New York Times,* Jan. 21, 1998.

Reed, D., and Sork, T. J. "Ethical Considerations in Distance Education." *American Journal of Distance Education,* 1990, *4*(2), 30–43.

Schrum, L., and Harris, J. "Ethical Electronic Research: Creating a Dialogue." Paper presented at the Qualitative Interest Group International Conference. University of Georgia, Athens, Jan. 1996.

Shaffer, C. R., and Anundsen, K. *Creating Community Anywhere: Finding Support and Connection in a Fragmented World.* New York: Putnam, 1993.

Weber, T. E. "Does Anything Go? Limiting Free Speech on the Net." *Wall Street Journal,* Dec. 8, 1997, p. R29.

Winner, L. "Who Will Be in Cyberspace?" [http://www.lanl.gov/SFC/95]. Paper presented at the 1995 Conference on Society and the Future of Computing, Durango, Colo., June 11–14, 1995.

MARGARET E. HOLT is associate professor of adult education at the University of Georgia, Athens, and an associate with the Charles F. Kettering Foundation.

Common themes and practical guidelines from the previous chapters
are summarized, and some implications of emerging technologies for
adult learning are considered.

Adult Learning and the Internet: Themes and Things to Come

Brad Cahoon

The changes the Internet has produced in the lives of teachers and learners have been so rapid and so radical that slowing down to reflect on their implications can be difficult. New trends and technologies seem to flash before us with each click of the mouse, and in our anxiety to keep pace we may neglect to pause and consider what has already been achieved. The vertiginous pull of real and imagined futures can hinder our ability to reflect and plan.

Collectively, the chapters in this sourcebook provide a cross-section of the current state of the art in Internet-based adult and continuing education. In this concluding chapter, I examine some themes that have emerged throughout the sourcebook that may help adult educators make good use of the Internet.

Adult Learners on the Internet

Millions of adults have learned to use e-mail and the Web, and Internet skills seem sure to become an increasingly common aspect of work and private life as we enter the twenty-first century. As I observe in Chapter One, relatively few Internet users have had the benefit of formal instruction, with the majority relying on self-directed learning and informal knowledge sharing within work groups to master client software. Understanding the personal factors that influence adults' acquisition of Internet skills can help educators make more effective use of these technologies.

Several of the authors of this volume note that adults' experiences with the Internet are consistent with the conventional wisdom about the characteristics of adult learners: the importance of life experiences and social situations in motivating their learning; their need to apply learning quickly to practical tasks; their ability to pursue self-directed learning; and their struggles to balance learning projects against the constraints of time, space, economic resources, and personal relationships. These familiar concepts are all valuable heuristics in the study of adult learning on the Internet.

For both recreational and professional users of the Internet, social relationships are powerful motivators. Adults of all ages are drawn to the new communicative channels of e-mail, on-line conferencing, and Web publishing by their desire to interact with others. Similarly, their need for fast solutions to the intellectual problems raised by their work helps account for the effectiveness of the electronic performance support systems (EPSS) that Gilbert describes in Chapter Two.

The use of an EPSS for on-demand work information illustrates how Internet technologies are changing the nature of knowledge-intensive tasks and thus the need for adult learning. The ability to search and refer to deep, specialized information resources makes it necessary to reconsider the value of some forms of learning. In an environment marked by increasing information overload, Gilbert suggests, one of the greatest benefits of intranets may be their ability to reduce learning needs, by prosthetically extending workers' stores of conceptual and procedural knowledge and thus allowing them to focus more attention on higher-order cognitive processes such as reflection. However, while the distribution of labor between humans and computers is constantly shifting, adults in the networked office are working harder than ever, and their learning is still strongly driven by their need to perform tasks and resolve work-related "cognitive press" (Bikson, 1987).

Self-direction is another familiar characteristic of adult learning that seems to be important both for the acquisition of basic Internet skills and for successful participation in Internet-based distance learning. In Chapter Six, Schrum indicates that students in on-line courses reported successful experiences when they were strongly motivated to participate, moved quickly through activities, had some prior computer experience, and felt comfortable directing their own learning. Even the most basic forms of Internet instruction, such as the Type I courses described by Eastmond in Chapter Four, can foster self-directed learning by encouraging the independent exploration of Internet resources. However, not all adult students enjoy the autonomy of on-line environments. In Chapter Five, Holt and her coauthors cite examples of students who felt frustrated and isolated by the lack of familiar social cues. These learners experienced the construction of knowledge primarily as a shared activity, guided by the give-and-take of discourse.

Several of the authors note the benefits of the Internet for adult learners struggling with time and access constraints. Faced with the need to reconcile learning with the demands of employers, spouses, children, and others, adult students require flexible scheduling and the ability to complete work independently. Whether or not their personal learning styles are strongly self-directed, nontraditional students are increasingly demanding the flexibility of Internet-based instruction.

Internet-Based Distance Education

The chapters by Eastmond, Holt and her coauthors, and Schrum present a composite picture of current Internet-based distance education. The courses described by these authors reflect new forms of collaborative learning, but also show how the same factors that can make such courses stimulating for students present instructors with unusual challenges.

E-mail, Web-based conferencing, and student publication of Web pages all help to enable group learning activities, whether the students also participate in face-to-face sessions or are geographically dispersed. Communicating and working together on the Internet can be difficult for some learners and hard to coordinate for instructors. In Chapter Six, Schrum warns of the need for instructors to consider new strategies for group formation, since students can find it difficult to assess each other's work styles without face-to-face meetings.

On-line discussion is singled out by several of the authors as a powerful tool for the development of critical thinking and deliberative skills. The dependence of current conferencing technologies on writing challenges students to reflect more deeply on their ideas as they try to articulate them effectively. On-line discussions have the potential to be more inclusive than face-to-face meetings, where discourse tends to be dominated by the most vocal participants. But as Holt and her coauthors demonstrate in their comparison of mailing lists and Web-based conferencing, on-line discussion can lapse into incoherence unless the technology used provides a clear visual and temporal organization of the participants' contributions.

Eastmond and Holt both note that the effective instructional use of on-line discussions places new requirements on instructors for skillful facilitation. In the absence of body language and other social cues of face-to-face instruction, the instructor must work harder to guide the discussion process and to help the group create a sense of community. To keep discussions on track without unduly influencing them, instructors may need to adopt a more objective, disinterested persona on occasions when they intervene in the flow of conversation. Private e-mail is also critical in monitoring progress and keeping all participants engaged.

Creating Distance Learning Courses

In Chapter Three, King points out that organizational support for the creation of Web-based instructional resources is often limited but that instructors can and should create such resources themselves. Even in those rare instances where an institution provides strong instructional design support, instructors must be prepared to collaborate on matters of content and curriculum. The practical guidelines provided by King can help any instructor begin to develop his or her own Web resources.

Like the EPSS design process described by Gilbert, creating Web-based instruction is an iterative process requiring preliminary assessment, the construction and testing of materials, and a commitment to revision and maintenance.

Research cited by Schrum suggests that creating a full-scale on-line course can take two or three times as long as the creation of a traditional course. However, King provides several examples of simple Web projects that can be developed quickly to supplement face-to-face instruction.

Schrum identifies several areas of concern in repurposing activities from traditional courses for use in distance learning. Instructors must evaluate what resources are necessary to complete the activity, how it will support interaction between students and the instructor, and how its progress and completion will be monitored.

On-Line Teaching and Learning as Research

Several of the authors describe on-line courses that also functioned as research projects. While such research designs may raise questions about both reliability and instructional value, this phenomenon seems a natural extension of the fact that educators are learning how to teach on the Internet as they go along. As Holt comments in Chapter Seven, such research raises ethical issues of informed consent, but the failure to study and publish the results of practice also raises concerns about whether educators are doing their best to understand and share their knowledge of these fast-moving technologies. As more institutions pursue the development of on-line courses, it becomes increasingly vital that instructors collect and analyze data and share the results of their teaching experiences with their peers.

The collaboration of students and teachers as research partners is also an example of the ways in which the Internet is restructuring the lines of status and control that have defined traditional schooling. Citing Duchastel (1996–97), Schrum describes an emerging pedagogy that invites us to move from a concept of schooling based on static content and goals to a focus on the shared process of constructing meaning.

These challenges to prevailing paradigms suggest exhilarating new possibilities for the organization of education, but we should heed the warning of Holt in Chapter Seven and avoid the automatic equation of technological advances with progress. The new paradigms will still involve problems of honesty, privacy and confidentiality, and, crucially, of equitable access. Much more research on on-line instruction, especially longitudinal studies tracking students and courses over time, will be necessary to understand the advantages and disadvantages of Internet-based instruction.

Institutional Issues

The number of traditional providers of adult and continuing education offering Internet-based courses is constantly growing. But while the Internet provides these institutions with access to new audiences, it also presents them with new competition from private training enterprises, publishers, and other for-profit organizations. The success of traditional providers in this new arena will depend largely on their ability to deliver the levels of administrative support and customer service that characterize what Eastmond calls the "virtual institution," the most sophisticated model of Internet-based instruction. Robust systems for on-line registration, advisement, records management, and book purchasing will be essential to large-scale efforts to recreate colleges and universities as virtual institutions. Skillful technical support for both students and faculty will become indispensable.

As Schrum notes, administrators will have to make policy decisions about open or fixed-schedule enrollments and about acceptable class sizes. Like instructors, they will have to take risks, make mistakes, and learn from their failures. One of the most challenging tasks they will face will be the revision of standards for tenure and other incentives to reward faculty innovators. Whether higher education will navigate these obstacles successfully, or whether instead it will become an increasingly marginalized force in a new educational marketplace, remains to be seen.

Conclusion: Things to Come

Imagining the future, we can be certain only that the Internet will continue to evolve and that each technological innovation will create new demands and opportunities for adult learning. The on-line learning environments of the next decade are likely to be shaped more by social and economic forces than by the efforts of researchers. However, some new directions have already become visible.

The number of adults on the Internet will continue to grow as personal computers become cheaper and as the entertainment media drive the widespread availability of faster network connectivity. Full-motion video and CD-quality audio will eventually become the norm for personal computers on the Internet, and with them the general use of desktop videoconferencing.

Improvements in speech recognition and alternative input devices will probably be significant in making computers and the Internet more accessible to adults who cannot work effectively with on-screen text. Nonetheless, literacy will remain a serious barrier to Internet use for many.

Long-standing research efforts in intelligent tutoring systems (Wenger, 1987) could be used to make Web-based instruction smarter. Such systems would rely on knowledge bases to do simple reasoning about their content domains and about students' preferences and progress.

Learning systems are also likely to become highly distributed. As bandwidth and processing power become more widely available and as development tools become more capable, distinctions between client and server computers will become less clear-cut. It will be commonplace for students and instructors to operate personal Web servers and for software agents to carry out exchanges of course-related information on behalf of both.

It is also likely that various virtual reality technologies, whether based on desktop computers, headsets, or immersive rooms, will provide virtual spaces for students to explore course content and approximate face-to-face interactions with other students and with teachers.

While these examples may appear fanciful, the technology to support all of them is already well developed in 1998, and in many instances their costs are approaching the price and performance thresholds necessary for widespread use. It is far more difficult to speculate about the social changes that might coincide with the emergence of these technologies.

Those who have observed firsthand the relative availability of Internet resources in rich and poor communities are unlikely to question the claim that an information underclass is already coming into being in the United States. How wide this gap between haves and have-nots will become in the future will depend on technology costs and especially on the success of attempts to use the Internet as an instrument for the reform and revitalization of public education. At issue is not the number of computers in schools, but how effectively educational institutions will help develop the skills of critical Internet use in the wider society.

References

Bikson, T. K. "Cognitive Press in Computer-Mediated Work." In G. Salvendy, S. L. Sauter, and J. J. Hurrell, Jr. (eds.), *Social, Ergonomic, and Stress Aspects of Work with Computers.* New York: Elsevier, 1987.

Duchastel, P. "A Web-Based Model for University Instruction." *Journal of Educational Technology Systems,* 1996–97, 25(3), 221–228.

Wenger, E. *Artificial Intelligence and Tutoring Systems: Computational Approaches to the Communication of Knowledge.* Los Altos, Calif.: Morgan Kaufmann, 1987.

BRAD CAHOON is the Webmaster and coordinator of computer instruction at the University of Georgia Center for Continuing Education, Athens.

Index

Abramson, J., 46, 49
Access: as benefit of Internet, 72; as ethical concern, 63, 67–68, 76; new technologies for, 75; and Web-based course development, 28
Active learning, 34, 35
Adams, G., 46, 50
Adult learners: characteristics of, 2, 21, 29, 34; and Internet-based distance education, 33–40, 72, 73–74; and Internet-based education, 71–76; and intranets, 20–21, 72; progress of, in Internet courses, 39–40; and Web-based course development, 29, 35–36, 38–39, 73–74
"Adult Learning and the Internet" Web site, University of Georgia Center for Continuing Education, 2
Alessi, S. M., 17, 22
ALNTALK, 65–66
"Alternative Teaching Methods" Web course, 25–26
American Internet User Survey, 1997, 67
Anderson, J. R., 8, 13
Anderson, T. D., 45, 49
Andragogical principals, 29
Anonymity, 65
Anundsen, K., 44–45, 50, 67, 69
Ashworth, R. L., 59, 60
Assessment: in on-line discussion forums, 47–48, 67; of on-line instruction, 56–57; Web-based, 27
Assignment submission: with e-mail, 27; on Web sites, 27
Associative linking, 7
Asynchronicity, 35, 37, 54, 57

Baron, J. P., 19, 20, 23
Bikson, T. K., 72, 76
Bly, S. A., 55, 60
Bobrow, D. G., 55, 61
Boise State University, 58
Bolles, R. N., 68
Boshuizen, H.P.A., 17, 21, 22
Boston, R. L., 54, 60
Brandt, D. S., 7, 12
Brookfield, S., 46, 49
Brown, J. S., 21, 22

Bullock, C. D., 65–66, 68
Burge, E. J., 37, 38, 40

Caffarella, R. S., 34, 41
Cahoon, B., 1–3, 5, 6, 9, 12, 71, 76
Career advancement, 67
Carroll, J. M., 11, 12
Cearley, K., 26, 29, 31
CGI (Common Gateway Interface) programs, 27
Clark, R. C., 20, 21, 22
Class (group) size, 58, 75
Clemente, P. C., 67, 69
Client-server model, 7–8
Cognition and Technology Group at Vanderbilt, 17, 22
Collaborative learning, 34–35, 37, 55, 57, 74. See also Group learning
Collins, A., 21, 22
Computer conferencing. See On-line conferencing
Computer skill learning, 6–7. See also Internet skill learning and teaching
Computer-based training, 17, 18
Computer-mediated communication (CMC), 44–45, 53, 54–55
Conferencing. See On-line conferencing
Confidentiality, 65
Conklin, E. J., 7, 12
Constructivist learning, 36
Cook, D. L., 36, 40
Course development on the World Wide Web, 25–31, 54; adult learning and, 29, 35–36, 38–39, 73–74; advanced options for, 27–28; basic options for, 26–27; bells and whistles for, 28; curriculum development and, 29; evaluation of, 29–30, 59; guidelines for, 28–30, 55–60; institutional issues of, 59, 74–75; organizational issues of, 58–59; pedagogical issues of, 56–57; technological issues in, 28–29; Web site construction for, 29; Web site design for, 30–31. See also Internet-based courses; Internet-based distance education; On-line courses
Credit, 59
Critical thinking skills, 45, 46, 47–48

77

Ordering Information

NEW DIRECTIONS FOR ADULT AND CONTINUING EDUCATION is a series of paperback books that explores issues of common interest to instructors, administrators, counselors, and policy makers in a broad range of adult and continuing education settings—such as colleges and universities, extension programs, businesses, the military, prisons, libraries, and museums. Books in the series are published quarterly in Spring, Summer, Fall, and Winter and are available for purchase by subscription and individually.

SUBSCRIPTIONS cost $54.00 for individuals (a savings of 35 percent over single-copy prices) and $90.00 for institutions, agencies, and libraries. Standing orders are accepted. New York residents, add local sales tax for subscriptions. (For subscriptions outside the United States, add $7.00 for shipping via surface mail or $25.00 for air mail. Orders must be prepaid in U.S. dollars by check drawn on a U.S. bank or charged to VISA, MasterCard, or American Express.)

SINGLE COPIES cost $22.00 plus shipping (see below) when payment accompanies order. California, New Jersey, New York, and Washington, D.C., residents, please include appropriate sales tax. Canadian residents, add GST and any local taxes. Billed orders will be charged shipping and handling. No billed shipments to post office boxes. (Orders from outside the United States must be prepaid in U.S. dollars by check drawn on a U.S. bank or charged to VISA, MasterCard, or American Express.)

SHIPPING (SINGLE COPIES ONLY): $30.00 and under, add $5.50; to $50.00, add $6.50; to $75.00, add $7.50; to $100.00, add $9.00; to $150.00, add $10.00.

ALL PRICES are subject to change.

DISCOUNTS FOR QUANTITY ORDERS are available. Please write to the address below for information.

ALL ORDERS must include either the name of an individual or an official purchase order number. Please submit your order as follows:
  Subscriptions: specify series and year subscription is to begin
  Single copies: include individual title code (such as ACE 59)

MAIL ALL ORDERS TO:
Jossey-Bass Publishers
350 Sansome Street
San Francisco, CA 94104–1342

Phone subscriptions or single-copy orders toll-free at (888) 378–2537 or at (415) 433–1767 (toll call).
Fax orders toll-free to: (800) 605–2665.

FOR SUBSCRIPTION SALES OUTSIDE OF THE UNITED STATES, contact any international subscription agency or Jossey-Bass directly.